The The Storage Networking
would like to thank th
for making this version o

www.cisco.com/go/storagenetworking

Computer Associates®

www.ca.com/brightstor

www.equallogic.com

www.hp.com/storage

www.ibm.com/storage

www.intel.com/design/intarch/
platforms/storage/index.htm

If your organization is a SNIA member and interested in sponsoring
the 2006/2007 edition of this dictionary, please contact
Derek Jenkins at Derek.Jenkins@snia.org

Storage Networking Industry Association

500 Sansome Street, Suite 504
San Francisco, CA 94111
Phone: 415-402-0006

www.snia.org

ᴜnary of Storage Networking Terminology

ᴏrage networking-related terms and the Definitions applied to them
by the Storage Networking Industry Association

The members of the Storage Networking Industry Association (SNIA) have collaborated to create this Dictionary of Storage and Storage Networking Terminology. This collaboration stands as a monument representing the dedication of the SNIA members to create and deliver standards and educational materials for the Storage Industry. In the creation of this Dictionary, we have utilized our members extensive knowledge of the industry to define the terms and acronyms used in the Storage Industry. This dictionary thus represents the storage networking industry's most comprehensive attempt to date to arrive at a common body of terminology for the technologies it represents.

The reader should recognize that in this rapidly evolving field, new terminology is constantly being introduced, and common usage is shifting. The SNIA regards this dictionary as a living document, to be updated as necessary to reflect a consensus on common usage, and encourages readers to treat it in that spirit. Comments and suggestions for improvement are gratefully accepted at any time, with the understanding that any submission of comments or suggestions contributes them to SNIA; and SNIA will own all rights (including any copyright or intellectual property rights) in them. Comments and suggestions should be directed to dictionary@snia.org or education@snia.org.

Most of the terms in this dictionary have meaning primarily in specific sub-contexts of storage networking, such as SCSI or Storage Systems. Wherever this is true, the primary context(s) for the term is(are) noted between the term itself and its definition. Terms that do not have one or more contexts identified are generally applicable to the data processing industry.

The SNIA hereby grants permission for individuals to use this glossary for personal use only, and for corporations and other business entities to use this glossary for internal use only (including internal copying, distribution, and display) provided that:

1. Any definition reproduced must be reproduced in its entirety with no alteration, and,

2. Any document, printed or electronic, in which material from this glossary (or any portion hereof) is reproduced must acknowledge the SNIA copyright on that material, and must credit the SNIA for granting permission for its reuse.

Other than as explicitly provided above, you may not make any commercial use of this glossary, sell any or all of this glossary, or distribute this glossary to third parties. All rights not explicitly granted above are expressly reserved to (by?) SNIA. In particular, the provisions above do not grant the rights to make any commercial use of this glossary, sell any or all of this dictionary, or distribute this dictionary to third parties.

Permission to use this glossary for purposes other than those enumerated above may be requested by e-mailing education@snia.org; please include the identity of the requesting individual and/or company and a brief description of the purpose, nature, and scope of the requested use.

Copyright © 2005 Storage Networking Industry Association. Last updated on September 1, 2005.

Key Websites

- www.snia.org - This is the official SNIA website
- www.snia.org/education - SNIA Education
- www.snia.org/news/events/ - SNIA and Industry Calendar of Events
- www.snia.org/education/certification/ - The SNIA Storage Networking Certification Program
- www.storagenetworkingworld.com* - Website for Storage Networking World events
- www.snia.org/smi/home - SNIA's Storage Management Initiative
- www.snia.org/tech_center - SNIA Technology Center
- www.snia.org/tech_activities/dmf/ - SNIA Data Management Forum
- www.snia.org/ipstorage/home - SNIA IP Storage Forum
- www.snia.org/smi/home/ - SNIA Storage Management Forum
- www.snia.org/tech_activities/storage_security - SNIA Storage Security Industry Forum

SNIA Worldwide

- www.snia-europe.org - SNIA Europe
- www.snia-j.org - SNIA Japan
- www.snia.org.cn - SNIA China
- www.snia.org.au - SNIA Australia/New Zealand
- www.snia-sa.org - SNIA South Asia
- www.snia-india.org - SNIA India
- www.snia.ca - SNIA Canada

Important Dates to Remember

Storage Networking World Europe*
September 5-6, 2006 - Messe Frankfurt
www.snweurope.com

Storage Networking World*
October 24-27, 2005 - Orlando, FL
www.snwusa.com

Enterprise Information World**
December 5-8, 2005 - Meadowlands, NJ
www.enterpriseinformationworld.com

SNIA Winter Symposium
January 24-27, 2006 - San Jose, CA
www.snia.org/events

Storage Networking World*
April 3-6, 2006 - San Diego, CA
www.snwusa.com

SNIA Summer Symposium
June 26-30, 2006 - Boston, MA
www.snia.org/events

Developer Solutions Conference and Showcase
September 18-22, 2006 - San Jose, CA
www.DeveloperSolutions.org

Storage Networking World*
October 30 - November 2, 2006 - Orlando, FL
www.snwusa.com

*co-owned and produced by SNIA with Computerworld
** owned and produced by SNIA

To learn more about additional events that SNIA is participating in, please visit www.snia.org/events

SNIA Technology Center

"The Center of Excellence for Storage Networking"

The SNIA Technology Center, located in Colorado Springs, CO, hosts programs that accelerate the development and introduction of advanced network storage technologies and solutions. The 14,000 sq. ft. facility provides programs and educational offerings to support end-users, integrators, and member company employees. As the venue of choice for SNIA programs, the Technology Center supports SNIA members to work collaboratively in developing technologies, standards, and tests that enable more efficient, complete, and trusted networked storage infrastructures. The Tech Center is also involved in the pre-staging and hosting of events and activities worldwide.

The Technology Center currently hosts educational courses for storage networking, standards-based interoperability programs, qualification of supported multi-vendor solutions, proof-of-concept testing, and conformance to standards qualification tests, all of which accelerate the delivery of the goals and milestones of the SNIA. In just a few years, the SNIA Technology Center has become the venue of choice for storage industry vendors, partners, and end users to receive education and to collaborate to deliver end-user requested technologies and solutions to the marketplace.

For more information about the Technology Center and a complete list of program offerings, visit the Web site at www.snia.org/tech_center/

SNIA Technology Center
301 Rockrimmon Blvd South
Colorado Springs, CO 80919 USA
Tel: +1.719.884.8902
Fax: +1.719.884.8912

SNIA Education

Accelerate Your Learning Curve

The SNIA Education offers curricula and courses for the end-user, integrator and vendor communities at the Technology Center as well as other locations. The offerings are vendor-neutral and help individuals develop and deploy more effective storage solutions through better understanding of storage practices, technologies, and standards. some courses are taught at the SNIA Technology Center in Colorado Springs, and include extensive hands-on lab access to the Technology Center hardware and software infrastructure.

For end-users, courses provide the knowledge and hands-on experience to help you make smarter storage investments, get the most out of your existing storage infrastructures, and save you time and money by avoiding blind alleys and other pitfalls.

For vendors, courses provide the solid foundational knowledge to help accelerate development efforts. For customer facing personnel (Sales, Professional Services, Field Services, Product Managers), the courses provide the foundational through in-depth knowledge required to plan, design, implement, support, and troubleshoot flexible storage architectures and designs.

In addition to being a credible, vendor-neutral source of information, the SNIA hosts the industry's interoperability and development lab facilities. SNIA and the Technology Center offer an excellent platform for much needed, vendor-neutral, hands-on education options.

For more information, visit the website at http://www.snia.org/education/courses.

SNIA Networking Certification Program (SNCP)

Overview

The SNIA Storage Networking Certification Program (SNCP) provides a strong foundation of vendor-neutral, systems-level credentials that integrate with and complement individual vendor certifications. The structure of the SNCP has been enhanced to reflect the advancement and growth of storage networking technologies over the past few years, and to provide for expanded offerings in the future. Through evolving and enhancing the SNCP, the SNIA is establishing a uniform standard by which individual knowledge and skill sets can be judged.

Why Certification?

For professionals, certification through the SNIA SNCP is validation of an individual's level of storage networking knowledge and expertise.

- Validate your skills and knowledge
- Gain peer recognition
- Make yourself more valuable to your company
- Target and build upon the skills you have as an industry professional

For organizations, SNIA SNCP certification will provide employers with a benchmark against which to measure employees' skills. The SNCP will provide a level of assurance that employees have the requisite skills and abilities to support the deployment of storage networks.

- The updated program is designed to reduce certification overlap by leveraging common vendor, reseller and end-user goals
  - For vendors, SNIA exams are integrated into vendor programs and vice versa save time, effort, and money for the vendor, reseller and end-user
  - Resellers can now leverage vendor neutral credentials in promoting storage networking operations and/or services
  - And individuals will be able to leverage a SNIA exam or credential into multiple vendor programs

SNIA 2006 Certification Credentials

- SNIA Certified Professional (SCP) 2006
- SNIA Certified Systems Engineer (SCSE) 2006
- SNIA Certified Architect (SCA) 2006
- SNIA Certified Storage Networking Expert (SCSN-E) 2006

For more information on the program updates, please visit www.snia.org/education/certification.

The SNIA Qualified Sales Professional 2005 program for Storage Networking and IT Sales Professionals is now available!!!

This new Qualification credential is now available and can be obtained by successfully passing the new SNIA Qualified Sales Professional on-line (web-based) test. This test is available to take at your personal workstation over the internet! The test length is between 37 to 45 questions and you have up to three hours to complete the test.

Please go to http://ibt.prometric.com/snia to take the test.

This is an on-line non-proctored test designed for the Storage Sales Networking Professional or those IT Sales Professionals who are entering this area. The test is designed to be informative and will be updated frequently to meet the needs of the SNIA Qualified Sales Professional participant.

For the successful candidate, they will receive the use of the SQSP 2005 logo and a certificate (pdf). Since it is a non-proctored test, it will not count towards SNIA Certification.

For more information on the program updates, please visit www.snia.org/education/certification.

SNIA End User Council

The EUC was created by end users for end users to share ideas, address management challenges and advance development of storage solutions that deliver business value.. All end users of storage networking solutions not involved with the sales, marketing, engineering, or manufacturing of storage networking products are invited to join!

EUC membership is open exclusively and free to storage end users so sign up now! For more information and an application please visit http://advisorygroups.snia.org/home/#euc.

SNIA-Conformance Testing Program (SNIA-CTP)

Developed, owned and operated by the SNIA, the SNIA-CTP consists of master test suites designed to test the compliance of a vendor's Storage Management Initiative-Specification (SMI-S) implementation to one or more of the specification's profiles. The result: Customers can purchase products built using a tested and standardized interface, which will aid in the deployment of multi-vendor storage management environments.

Product testing takes place at the vendor-neutral SNIA Technology Center, whose classrooms and laboratory facilities are designed to provide access to state-of-the-art resource and equipment for interoperability testing.

For more information, go to http://www.snia.org/tech_activities/snia-ctp/.

FarSighted - *News and information for storage professionals*

www.FarSightedNews.org

FarSighted is the Storage Networking Industry Association's online newsletter providing news and information from across the storage networking industry, presented in one convenient, online publication.

FarSighted, offers readers can't-find-it-elsewhere articles and analysis, access to top storage-focused stories from leading IT publications, book reviews, listings of upcoming events, and more. FarSighted also recaps everything happening at the Storage Networking Industry Association (SNIA), the organization helping to drive the entire storage networking industry's evolution.

To subscribe for a free monthly issue of FarSighted, visit www.FarSightedNews.org

FarSighted also offers Job Posting, Advertisement, and Sponsorship opportunities. If you are interested in any of these opportunities contact Derek Jenkins at Derek.Jenkins@snia.org.

TERMS AND ACRONYMS

access
CONTEXT [Security]

> The opportunity to make use of an information system resource.

access control
CONTEXT [File System] [Security]

> The granting or withholding of a service or access to a resource to a requestor based on the identity of the principal for which the requestor is acting.

access control list
CONTEXT [File System] [Security]

> A persistent list that enumerates the rights of principals (e.g., users and groups of users) to access resources. Often used in file system context to denote a persistent list maintained by a file system and defining user and group permissions for file and directory access.

access control mechanism
CONTEXT [Security]

> A security safeguard designed to detect and deny unauthorized access and permit authorized access in an information system.

access fairness

CONTEXT [Fibre Channel]

A process by which nodes are guaranteed access to a Fibre Channel arbitrated loop independent of other nodes' activity.

access method

CONTEXT [Fibre Channel][Operating System]

1. The means used to access a physical transmission medium in order to transmit data.
2. (In IBM Corporation's OS/390 operating system and its precursors) A file organization method, such as sequential, random, indexed, etc., and the operating system software used to implement it.

access path

CONTEXT [Storage System]

The combination of host bus adapter, logical unit number, route through the host-storage interconnect, controller, and logical unit used by a computer to communicate with a storage device. Some configurations support multiple access paths to a single device. cf. multi-path I/O.

accountability

CONTEXT [Security]

The property enabling individuals' activities on a system to be linked back to them as individuals in such a way that there is little possibility for them to deny responsibility for them (see nonrepudiation).

ACL

CONTEXT [File System] [Security]

Acronym for access control list.

ACS

CONTEXT [Data Recovery]

Acronym for automated cartridge system.

active

CONTEXT [Fibre Channel]

The state of a Fibre Channel Sequence Initiator between the start of transmission of the first data frame of a sequence and the completion of transmission of the last data frame in the sequence. Also, the state of a Fibre Channel Sequence Recipient between the start of reception of the first data frame of a sequence and the completion of reception of the last data frame in the sequence.

active-active (components, controllers)

CONTEXT [Storage System]

Synonym for dual active components or controllers.

active copper

CONTEXT [Fibre Channel]

A type of Fibre Channel physical connection that allows up to 30 meters of copper cable between adjacent devices.

active-passive (components, controllers)

CONTEXT [Storage System]

Synonym for hot standby components or controllers.

active component

A system component that requires electrical power to operate. In a storage subsystem, for example, active components might include power supplies, storage devices, fans, and controllers. By contrast, enclosures and canisters are not normally active components.

adapter

A hardware device that converts the timing and protocol of one bus or interface to another. Adapters are typically implemented as specialized hardware on system boards, or as add-in cards, to enable a computer system's processing hardware to access peripheral devices. An example adapter is a host Bus Adapter. Adapter is the preferred term in Fibre Channel contexts. cf. adapter card, host bus adapter, network interface card, NIC.

adapter card

An adapter implemented as a printed circuit module.

adaptive array

CONTEXT [Storage System]

> A disk array that is capable of changing its algorithm for virtual data
> address to physical data location mapping dynamically (i.e., while the
> array is operating). AutoRAID from Hewlett-Packard, which can change
> a given virtual disk representation from mirrored to parity RAID, is an
> adaptive array.

address

CONTEXT [Storage Device] [Storage System][SCSI]

> 1. A fixed length bit pattern that uniquely identifies a block of data
>   stored on a disk or tape. Typically treated as a number to which a
>   mapping algorithm can be applied to determine the physical location
>   of a block of data. Applying this mapping algorithm to disk block
>   addresses yields the cylinder, head, and relative sector number at
>   which data may be found. Tape block addresses typically refer to the
>   relative position of a block of data in a single linear stream of blocks.
> 2. A fixed-length bit pattern that uniquely identifies a location (bit, byte,
>   word, etc.) in a computer memory.
> 3. [SCSI] A byte whose value uniquely identifies a device connected to
>   a SCSI bus for purposes of communication.

address identifier

CONTEXT [Fibre Channel]

> An address value used to identify the source (S_ID) or destination (D_ID)
> of a frame. The FC-SW standard includes a table of special address
> identifier values and their meanings.

address resolution

CONTEXT [Network]

> The process of determining a MAC address, given a more abstract LAN
> or WAN address.

Address Resolution Protocol

CONTEXT [Network]

1. Any protocol used to obtain a mapping from a higher layer address to a lower layer address. Abbreviated ARP. The Acronym ARP is most often used to refer to the Ethernet Address Resolution Protocol (below)
2. The protocol used by an IP networking layer to map IP addresses to lower level hardware (i.e., MAC) addresses. There are four ARP messages for IP running over Ethernet: arp requests and replies and reverse arp request and replies.

addressing

CONTEXT [Storage System]

An algorithm by which areas of fixed disk, removable cartridge media, or computer system main memory are uniquely identified. cf. block addressing, C-H-S addressing, explicit addressing, implicit addressing

administration host

CONTEXT [Network]

A computer that manages one or more storage subsystems (e.g., filers, disk array subsystems, tape subsystems, etc.)

administrator

A person charged with the installation, configuration, and management of a computer system, network, storage subsystem, database, or application.

advanced encryption standard

CONTEXT [Security]

A cryptographic algorithm designated by NIST as a replacement for DES. Abbreviated AES. The actual algorithm selected is also known as Rijndael.

Advanced Intelligent Tape

CONTEXT [Storage Device]

A tape device and media technology introduced by Sony Corporation.

Advanced Technology Attachment

Advanced Technology Attachment is a standard designed to connect hard and removable disk drives. It is the official name for Integrated Drive Electronics (IDE). Acronym ATA.

AES
CONTEXT [Security]

Acronym for advanced encryption standard.

agent

A program that performs one or more services (such as gathering information from the Internet), acting for or as a principal.

aggregation
CONTEXT [Network] [Storage System]

The combining of multiple similar and related objects or operations into a single one. Several disk or tape data streams are sometimes aggregated into a single stream for higher performance. Two or more disks can be aggregated into a single virtual disk for increased capacity. Two or more disks can be aggregated into a RAID array for high availability. Two or more I/O requests for adjacently located data can be aggregated into a single request to minimize request processing overhead and rotational latency. cf. consolidation.

AH
CONTEXT [Security]

Acronym for authentication header.

AIT
CONTEXT [Storage Device]

Acronym for advanced intelligent tape.

algorithmic mapping
CONTEXT [Storage System]

Use of an algorithm to translate from one data addressing domain to another. If a volume is algorithmically mapped, the physical location of a block of data may be calculated from its virtual volume address using known characteristics of the volume (e.g. stripe depth and number of member disks). cf. dynamic mapping, tabular mapping

alias

An alternate name for an entity that is more easily human readable. Aliases are sometimes used for grouping purposes, e.g. alias address identifier in Fibre Channel.

alias address identifier

CONTEXT [Fibre Channel]

> One or more address identifiers which may be recognized by an N_Port in addition to its N_Port Identifier. Alias address identifiers are used to form groups of N_Ports so that frames may be addressed to a group rather than to individual N_Ports. cf. hunt group, multicast group

AL_PA

CONTEXT [Fibre Channel]

> Acronym for Arbitrated Loop Physical Address.

alternate client restore

CONTEXT [Data Recovery]

> The process of restoring files to a different client than the one from which they were backed up.

alternate path restore

CONTEXT [Data Recovery]

> The process of restoring files to a different directory than the one from which they were backed up.

always on

CONTEXT [General][Fibre Channel]

> 1. The state of always having power applied (systems) or of being continually active (communication links).
> 2. [Fibre Channel] A state of always being powered on and/or continually active. In a Fibre Channel, ESCON, or Gigabit Ethernet context, "always on" describes the state of an operational link. It is constantly transmitting either data frames, idles or fill words. This can be contrasted with bursty transmissions and listening for a quiet line in Ethernet. For Fibre Channel management purposes being "always on" allows link level error detection on each transmitted word.

American National Standards Institute

> A coordinating organization for voluntary standards in the United States. Often abbreviated ANSI. The ANSI working committees most closely aligned with storage networking interests are called X3T10 (principally responsible for SCSI I/O interface standards), and X3T11 (principally responsible for Fibre Channel interface standards).

ANSI

Acronym for American National Standards Institute.

ANSI T10

The American National Standards Institute T10 technical committee, the standards organization responsible for SCSI standards for communication between computers and storage subsystems and devices.

ANSI T11

The American National Standards Institute T11 technical committee, the standards organization responsible for Fibre Channel and certain other standards for moving electronic data into and out of computers and intelligent storage subsystems and devices.

ANSI X3T10

The American National Standards Institute committee responsible for standards for accessing and controlling I/O devices. ANSI X3T10 is responsible for the SCSI family of standards. Often shortened to T10.

ANSI X3T11

The American National Standards Institute committee responsible for standards for high performance I/O interfaces such as Fibre Channel and HIPPI. Often shortened to T11.

API

Acronym for Application Programming Interface.

appliance

An intelligent device programmed to perform a single well-defined function, such as providing file, web, or print services. Appliances differ from general purpose computers in that their software is normally customized for the function they perform, pre-loaded by the vendor, and not alterable by the user. Appliances are generally considered to be capable of performing their specialized functions at lower cost and with higher reliability than general purpose servers. cf. filer.

application I/O request

application read request

application write request

CONTEXT [Storage System]

I/O requests made by storage clients, as distinguished from member I/O requests made by a storage subsystem's own control software. SNIA publications do not generally distinguish between I/O requests made by the operating environment (e.g., for paging, swapping, and file system directory lookups, etc.) and those made by user applications.

application programming interface

An interface used by an application program to request services. Abbreviated API. The term API is usually used to denote interfaces between applications and the software components that comprise the operating environment (e.g., operating system, file system, volume manager, device drivers, etc.)

application response measurement

An Open Group technical standard defining function calls for transaction monitoring. The ARM standard is being advanced in both The Open Group and the Distributed Management Task Force. The latter organization has defined an object oriented information model for describing units of work (i.e., transactions).

application specific integrated circuit

An integrated circuit designed for a particular application, such as interfacing to a SCSI bus. Acronym ASIC.

applications

Applications are any and all processes that can transform data into Information used by a Business Process. Applications can scale from desktop PDF file readers to federated applications spanning multiple databases and file systems throughout the enterprise.

arbitrated loop
CONTEXT [Fibre Channel]

1. A Fibre Channel interconnect topology in which each port is connected to the next, forming a loop. At any instant, only one port in a Fibre Channel Arbitrated Loop can transmit data. Before transmitting data, a port in a Fibre Channel Arbitrated Loop must participate with all other ports in the loop in an arbitration to gain the right to transmit data. The arbitration logic is distributed among all of a loop's ports.
2. The version of the Fibre Channel protocol used with the arbitrated loop physical topology.

arbitrated loop physical address
CONTEXT [Fibre Channel]

An 8-bit value used to identify a participating device in an Arbitrated Loop.

arbitration

Any process by which a user of a shared resource negotiates with other users for the (usually temporary) right to use the resource. A port connected to a shared bus must win arbitration before it transmits data on the bus.

archive
CONTEXT [Information Lifecycle Management]

1. (noun) A collection of data that is maintained as a long-term record of a business, application, or information state. Archives are typically kept for auditing, regulatory, analysis or reference purposes rather than for application or data recovery.
2. (verb) To copy or move data for purposes of retention; to create an archive(1).

ARM

1. Acronym for application response measurement.
2. A common microprocessor architecture, as well as the name of the company that created the architecture.

ARP
CONTEXT [Network]

Acronym for Address Resolution Protocol.

array

CONTEXT [Storage System]

A storage array, i.e., a disk array or tape array.

array configuration

CONTEXT [Storage System]

1. Assignment of the disks and operating parameters for a disk array. Disk array configuration includes designating the array's member disks or extents and the order in which they are to be used, as well as setting parameters such as stripe depth, RAID model, cache allowance, spare disk assignments, etc. cf. configuration, physical configuration.
2. The arrangement of disks and operating parameters that results from such an assignment.

ASIC

Acronym for Application Specific Integrated Circuit.

Association_Header

CONTEXT [Fibre Channel]

An optional header used to associate a Fibre Channel exchange with a process, system image, or multi-exchange I/O operation on an end system. May also be used as part of Exchange Identifier management.

assurance

CONTEXT [Security]

Process for demonstrating that the security goals and objectives for an IT product or system are met on a continuing basis.

assurance level

CONTEXT [Security]

The degree of confidence that a system will behave in accordance with its goals and objectives. The level of assurance obtained is generally related to the effort expended in analyzing the functioning of the system under both normal and unexpected conditions.

asymmetric cryptosystem

CONTEXT [Security]

A cryptographic algorithm in which different keys are used to encrypt and decrypt a single message or block of stored information. One of the keys is kept secret and referred to as a private key; the other key can be freely disclosed and is called a public key.

asymmetric virtualization

Synonym for out-of-band virtualization. Out-of-band virtualization is the preferred term.

asynchronous I/O request

CONTEXT [Storage Device] [Storage System]

A request to perform an asynchronous I/O operation.

asynchronous I/O operation

CONTEXT [Storage Device] [Storage System]

An I/O operation whose initiator does not await its completion before proceeding with other work. Asynchronous I/O operations enable an initiator to have multiple concurrent I/O operations in progress.

asynchronous replication

CONTEXT [Storage System]

A replication technique in which data must be committed to storage at only the primary site and not the secondary site before the write is acknowledged to the host. Data is then forwarded to the secondary site as the network capabilities permit.

Asynchronous Transfer Mode

CONTEXT [Network]

A connection-oriented data communications technology based on switching 53 byte fixed-length units of data called cells. Abbreviated ATM. Each cell is dynamically routed. ATM transmission rates are multiples of 51.840 Mbits per second. In the United States, a public communications service called SONET uses ATM at transmission rates of 155, 622, 2048, and 9196 Mbits per second. These are called OC-3, OC-12, OC-48, and OC-192 respectively. A similar service called SDH is offered in Europe. ATM is also used as a LAN infrastructure, sometimes with different transmission rates and coding methods than are offered with SONET and SDH. More information is available from the ATM Forum.

ATA

Acronym for Advanced Technology Attachment.

ATM

CONTEXT [Network]

Acronym for Asynchronous Transfer Mode.

atomic operation

An indivisible operation that, from an external perspective, occurs either in its entirety or not at all. For example, database management systems that implement the concept of business transactions treat each business transaction as an atomic operation on the database. This means that either all of the database updates that comprise a transaction are performed or none of them are performed; it is never the case that some of them are performed and others not. RAID arrays must implement atomic write operations to properly reproduce single-disk semantics from the perspective of their clients. Atomic operations are required to ensure that component failures do not corrupt stored data.

attack

CONTEXT [Security]

The act of trying to bypass security controls on a system.

attenuation

The power dissipation between an optical or electrical transmitter and a receiver. Expressed in units of decibels (dB).

audit trail

CONTEXT [Network][Security]

A chronological record of system activities that enables the reconstruction and examination of a sequence of events and/or changes in an object. The term audit trail may apply to information in an information system, to message routing in a communications system, or to any transfer of sensitive material and/or information.

authentication

CONTEXT [Network]

> The process of determining what principal a requestor or provider of services is or represents.

CONTEXT [Security]

> A security measure designed to establish the validity of a transmission, message, or originator, or a means of verifying an individual's authorization to receive information.

authentication header

CONTEXT[Security]

> A component of IPsec that permits the specification of various authentication mechanisms designed to provide connectionless integrity, data origin authentication, and an optional anti-replay service. Standardized by the Internet Engineering Task Force.

authenticity

CONTEXT [Security]

> The property that the identity of a subject or resource is the one claimed. Authenticity applies to entities such as users, processes, systems and information.

authorization

CONTEXT [Network] [Security]

> 1. [Network] The process of determining that a requestor is allowed to receive a service or perform an operation. Access control is an example of authorization.
> 2. [Security] The limiting of usage of information system resources to authorized users, programs, processes or other systems. Access control is a specific type of authorization. Authorization is formally described as controlling usage by subjects of objects.

auto swap

> Abbreviation for automatic swap . cf. cold swap, hot swap, warm swap.

automated cartridge system

CONTEXT [Data Recovery]

> Synonym for robot.

automatic backup

CONTEXT [Data Recovery]

A backup triggered by an event (e.g., a schedule point, or a threshold reached) rather than by human action.

automatic failover

Failover that occurs without human intervention.

automatic swap

The substitution of a replacement unit (RU) in a system for a defective one, where the substitution is performed by the system itself while it continues to perform its normal function (possibly at a reduced rate of performance). Automatic swaps are functional rather than physical substitutions, and do not require human intervention. Ultimately, however, defective components must be replaced in a physical hot, warm, or cold swap operation. cf. cold swap, hot swap, warm swap, hot spare.

automatic switchover

Synonym for automatic failover.

availability

The amount of time that a system is available during those time periods when it is expected to be available. Availability is often measured as a percentage of an elapsed year. For example, 99.95% availability equates to 4.38 hours of downtime in a year (0.0005 * 365 * 24 = 4.38) for a system that is expected to be available all the time. cf. data availability, high availability.

B

B_Port

CONTEXT [Fibre Channel]

The "Bridge" port within a bridge device used to extend a Fibre Channel inter-switch link. A B_Port connects only to an E_Port on a Fibre Channel switch.

B2D

CONTEXT [Data Recovery]

Acronym for Backup to Disk.

B2T

CONTEXT [Data Recovery]

Acronym for Backup to Tape.

backing store

Non-volatile memory. The term backing store is often used to contrast with cache, which is a (usually) volatile random access memory used to speed up I/O operations. Data held in a volatile cache must be replicated in or saved to a non-volatile backing store so that it can survive a system crash or power failure.

backup

CONTEXT [Data Recovery]

1. (noun) A collection of data stored on (usually removable) non-volatile storage media for purposes of recovery in case the original copy of data is lost or becomes inaccessible. Also called backup copy. To be useful for recovery, a backup must be made by copying the source data image when it is in a consistent state.
2. (noun) A process that creates a backup (definition 1).
3. (verb) The act of creating a backup. cf. archive.

backup client

CONTEXT [Data Recovery]

A computer system containing online data to be backed up.

backup copy

CONTEXT [Data Recovery]

A backup copy is a collection of data that constitutes a recoverable copy of a given set of data. Backup copies may require a restore in order to be usable. cf. replica

backup manager

CONTEXT [Data Recovery]

An application program whose purpose is to schedule and manage backup operations.

backup policy

CONTEXT [Data Recovery]

An IT installation's rules for how and when backup should be performed. Backup policies specify information such as which files or directories are to be backed up, the schedule on which backups should occur, which devices and media are eligible to receive the backups, how many copies are to be made, and actions to be performed if a backup does not succeed.

Backup to Disk

CONTEXT [Data Recovery]

Backup onto disk media. Acronym B2D.

Backup to Tape
CONTEXT [Data Recovery]

Backup onto tape media. Acronym B2T.

backup window
CONTEXT [Data Recovery]

An interval of time during which a set of data can be backed up without seriously affecting applications that use the data. For example, if an application accesses data from 8AM until midnight, then the window between midnight and 8AM is available for making backup copies. Offline backups require that applications not update data during the backup. Online backups typically use point in time copy technology to create consistent images of data for backup. If a backup uses different resources (storage devices, I/O paths, processing power) than the application, as is common with split mirror point-in-time copies, then the backup window is the time required to create the image. If the online backup shares resources with the applications using the data, as is common with copy-on-write point in time copies, the backup window may be increased due to resource contention.

bandwidth

1. The numerical difference between the upper and lower frequencies of a band of electromagnetic radiation.
2. Synonym for data transfer capacity.

basic input output system

A relatively small program that resides in programmable, non-volatile memory on a personal computer and that is responsible for booting that computer and performing certain operating system independent I/O operations. Abbreviated BIOS. Standard BIOS interrupts are defined to allow access to the computer's disk, video and other hardware components (for example, INT13 for disk access).

baud
CONTEXT [Network]

The maximum rate of signal state changes per second on a communications circuit. If each signal state change corresponds to a code bit, then the baud rate and the bit rate are the same. It is also possible for signal state changes to correspond to more than one code bit, so the baud rate may be lower than the code bit rate.

Bayonet Neil Councilman (connector)

CONTEXT [Network]

A type of coaxial cable connector sometimes used in Ethernet applications. Abbreviated BNC. The specification for BNC connectors is contained in EIA/TIA 403-A and MIL-C-39012.

BB_buffer

CONTEXT [Fibre Channel]

A buffer associated with buffer to buffer flow control.

BB_credit

CONTEXT [Fibre Channel]

Buffer-to-buffer credit; used to determine how many frames can be sent to a recipient when buffer to buffer flow control is in use.

beginning running disparity

CONTEXT [Fibre Channel]

The running disparity present at a transmitter or receiver when an ordered set is initiated.

BER

CONTEXT [Network] [Storage Device]

Acronym for Bit Error Rate.

Berkeley RAID Levels

CONTEXT [Storage System]

A family of disk array data protection and mapping techniques described by Garth Gibson, Randy Katz, and David Patterson in papers written while they were performing research into I/O subsystems at the University of California at Berkeley. There are six Berkeley RAID Levels, usually referred to by the names RAID Level 1, etc., through RAID Level 6. . cf. RAID 0, RAID 1, RAID 2, RAID 3, RAID 4, RAID 5, RAID 6.

best effort (class of service)

CONTEXT [Fibre Channel] [Network]

A class of service which does not guarantee delivery of packets, frames, or datagrams, but for which the network, fabric, or interconnect makes every reasonable delivery effort.

big endian

A format for the storage and transmission of binary data in which the most significant bits are stored at the numerically lowest addresses, or are transmitted first on a serial link.

BIOS

Acronym for basic input output system.

bit error rate

CONTEXT [Network] [Storage Device]

The probability that a transmitted bit will be erroneously received. Abbreviated BER. The BER is measured by counting the number of bits in error at the output of a receiver and dividing by the total number of bits in the transmission. BER is typically expressed as a negative power of 10.

bit synchronization

The process by which the receiver of a serial communication establishes its clocking used to locate code bits in a received data stream.

black

CONTEXT [Security]

A designation applied to information systems in the context of security analysis, and to associated areas, circuits, components, and equipment, in which sensitive information is not processed.

blind mating

The ability of pairs of components to be connected without the electrical or optical connection points being visible. Blind mating is usually accomplished by mechanical guides (e.g., slots and rails) on the components.

block

CONTEXT [Fibre Channel] [Storage Device] [Storage System]

1. The unit in which data is stored and retrieved on disk and tape devices. Blocks are the atomic unit of data recognition (through a preamble and block header) and protection (through a CRC or ECC).
2. A unit of application data from a single information category that is transferred within a single sequence.

block addressing

CONTEXT [Storage Device] [Storage System]

An algorithm for uniquely identifying blocks of data stored on disk or tape media by number, and then translating these numbers into physical locations on the media. cf. C-H-S addressing

block virtualization

The act of applying virtualization (q.v.), to one or more block based (storage) services for the purpose of providing a new aggregated, higher level, richer, simpler, secure etc. block service to clients. cf. file virtualization. Block virtualization functions can be nested. A disk drive, RAID system or volume manager all perform some form of block address to (different) block address mapping or aggregation.

BNC

CONTEXT [Network]

Acronym for Bayonet Neil Councilman, a type of Coaxial Cable Connector.

Specifications for BNC style connectors are defined in EIA/TIA 403-A and MIL-C-39012.

boot

booting

bootstrapping

The loading of code from a disk or other storage device into a computer's memory. Bootstrapping is an appropriate term since a code load typically occurs in steps, starting with a very simple program (BIOS) that initializes the computer's hardware and reads a sequence of data blocks from a fixed location on a pre-determined disk, into a fixed memory location. The data thus read is the code for the next stage of bootstrapping - usually an operating system loader. The loader completes the hardware setup and results in an executing operating system, in memory.

break mirror

CONTEXT [Storage System]

Remove a mirror component from the mirror, voiding its relationship with the other mirror components. The broken mirror component becomes a standalone volume in the system, and synchronization with the other mirror components is not maintained.

B

Bridge

CONTEXT [Fibre Channel]

1. A Fibre Channel Bridge pair provides a transparent fabric extension between two switch E_Ports through the use of 2 B_Ports tunneling through some alternative technology. The resulting Inter-Switch Link (ISL) "appears" to be a direct link between switches. For example, a bridge pair can take an incoming Fibre Channel frame from one B_Port on a Bridge, encapsulate that frame using FCIP (Fibre Channel over IP) and transmit the frame as payload over an IP network to the remote Bridge where the original frame is forwarded to the remote Fibre Channel Fabric switch E_Port through the remote Bridge's B_Port.

2. A Fibre Channel Bridge enables traffic carried along part of the path from a source device by Fibre Channel, (for example commands, blocks, status and control between a SCSI initiator or target source device) to be extended to the destination device using an alternative physical transport network technology (for example iSCSI or SCSI Bus). In some cases this "Bridge" is also referred to as a physical transport gateway, or storage router.

broadcast

CONTEXT [Fibre Channel] [Network]

The simultaneous transmission of a message to all receivers (ports) connected to a communication facility. Broadcast can be contrasted with unicast (sending a message to a specific receiver) and multicast (sending a message to select subset of receivers). In a Fibre Channel context, broadcast specifically refers to the sending of a message to all N_Ports connected to a fabric. cf. multicast, unicast

buffer

A solid state memory device or programming construct, used to hold data
momentarily as it moves along an I/O path or between software components.
Buffers allow devices to communicate using links with faster or slower
data transfer speeds, allow devices with different native processing
speeds to intercommunicate, and allow software components to intercommunicate, share data and coordinate their activities. cf. cache

buffer to buffer flow control

CONTEXT [Fibre Channel]

Flow control that occurs between two directly connected Fibre Channel
ports, e.g., an N_Port and its associated F_Port. A port indicates the number of frames buffers that can be sent to it (its buffer credit), before the
sender is required to stop transmitting and wait for the receipt of a "ready"
indication. Buffer to buffer flow control is used only when an NL-Local
port is logged into another NL-Local port, or when Nx ports are logged
into Fx ports.

bypass circuit

CONTEXT [Fibre Channel]

A circuit that automatically removes a device from a data path (such as a
Fibre Channel arbitrated loop) when valid signalling is lost.

byte

CONTEXT [Fibre Channel]

1. An eight-bit organizational unit for data.
2. The unit in which data is delivered to and by applications. In Fibre
    Channel, bytes are organized with the least significant bit denoted as
    bit 0 and most significant bit as bit 7. The most significant bit is shown
    on the left side in FC-PH documents, unless specifically indicated
    otherwise.

CA

CONTEXT [Security]

Acronym for certification authority

cable plant

All of an installation's passive communications elements (e.g., optical fibre, twisted pair, or coaxial cable, connectors, splices, etc.) between a transmitter and a receiver.

cache

A high speed memory or storage device used to reduce the effective time required to read data from or write data to a lower speed memory or device. Read cache holds data in anticipation that it will be requested by a client. Write cache holds data written by a client until it can be safely stored on more permanent storage media such as disk or tape. cf. buffer, disk cache, write back cache, write through cache

canister

CONTEXT [Storage System]

An enclosure for a single disk or tape. Canisters are usually designed to mount in shelves, which supply power, cooling, and I/O bus services to the devices. Canisters are used to minimize RF emissions and to simplify insertion and removal of devices in multi-device storage subsystems. cf. shelf

carousel

CONTEXT [Data Recovery]

> A media handling robot in which the media are stored in and selected from a rotating wheel.

carrier sense multiple access with collision detection

CONTEXT [Network]

> A physical layer data transmission protocol used in Ethernet and fast Ethernet networks. Abbreviated CSMA/CD. Carrier sense refers to arbitration for a shared link. Unlike "always on" physical protocols, carrier sense protocols require a node wishing to transmit to wait for the absence of carrier (indicating that another node is transmitting) on the link. Multiple access refers to the party line nature of the link. A large number of nodes (up to 500 in the case of Ethernet) share access to a single link. Collision detection refers to the possibility that two nodes will simultaneously sense absence of carrier and begin to transmit, interfering with each other. Nodes are required to detect this interference, and cease transmitting. In the case of Ethernet, each node detecting a collision is required to wait for a random interval before attempting to transmit again.

cascading

CONTEXT [Fibre Channel]

> The process of connecting two or more Fibre Channel hubs or switches together to increase the number of ports or extend distances.

catalog

CONTEXT [Data Recovery][File System]

> 1. [Data Recovery] A stored list of backed up files and directories and the locations (media identifiers) of the backup copies. Backup managers use catalogs to determine what files must be backed up, and to determine which media must be mounted and read to perform a restore.
> 2. [File System] A persistent data structure used by some file systems to keep track of the files they manage.

CC

CONTEXT [Security]

> Acronym for Common Criteria.

CDB
CONTEXT [SCSI]

> Acronym for Command Descriptor Block.

CDP
CONTEXT [Data Recovery]

> Acronym for Continuous Data Protection.

CDR
CONTEXT [Fibre Channel]

> Acronym for Clock and Data Recovery.

certificate
CONTEXT [Security]

> A data structure signed with a digital signature that is based a public key and asserts that the key belongs to a subject identified in the structure.

Certificate Revocation List
CONTEXT [Security]

> A time-stamped list of certificates that have been revoked by the Certification Authority. The CRL is signed by the issuing CA and is made available to entities that need to rely on a certificate for authentication. Acronym CRL.

certification authority
CONTEXT [Security]

> In a Public Key Infrastructure (PKI), the authority and organization responsible for issuing and revoking user certificates, and ensuring compliance with the PKI policies and procedures.

challenge
CONTEXT [Security]

> A step in an authentication dialog that must be answered using either a secret or process assumed to be known only by the other party. A challenge can be as simple as "What's your password?" or as complex as "Send me the result of a retinal scan of your right eye."

C

Challenge Handshake Authentication Protocol

CONTEXT [Security]

> A password-based authentication protocol that uses a challenge to verify that a user has access to a system. A hash of the supplied password with the challenge is sent for comparison so the cleartext password in never sent over the connection.

changed block

changed block point in time copy

CONTEXT [Storage System]

> Any of a class of point in time copy implementations or the resulting copies in which the copy and its source share storage for portions (usually blocks) of the copy that are not subsequently modified (in the source, or in the copy if the copy is writeable). Storage is physically copied only as a consequence of modifications (to the source, or to the copy if the copy is writeable). A changed block copy occupies only the storage necessary to hold the blocks of storage that have been changed since the point in time at which the copy logically occurred.

channel

1. [storage] The electrical circuits that sense or cause the state changes in recording media and convert between those state changes and electrical signals that can be interpreted as data bits.
2. [I/O] Synonym for I/O bus. The term channel has other meanings in other branches of computer technology. The definitions given here are commonly used when discussing storage and networking. cf. device channel, device I/O bus, I/O bus, host I/O bus

character

CONTEXT [Fibre Channel]

1. In general computing usage, synonym for byte.
2. A 10-bit information unit transmitted and received by FC-1. 8B/10B encoding provides the mapping between 8 bits of data and a 10 bit transmission character. Some transmission characters correspond to special codes and not all 10 bit sequences represent valid transmission characters.

character cell interface

Synonym for command line interface.

check data

CONTEXT [Storage System]

In a RAID array, data stored on member disks that can be used for regenerating any user data that becomes inaccessible.

checkpoint

CONTEXT [Data Recovery] [File System]

1. The recorded state of an application at an instant of time, including data, in-memory variables, program counter, and all other context that would be required to resume application execution from the recorded state.
2. An activity of a file system (such as the High Performance File System, HPFS, or the Andrews File System, AFS) in which cached meta data (data about the structures of the file system) is periodically written to the file system's permanent store. This allows the file system to maintain consistency if an unexpected stop occurs.

chunk

CONTEXT [Storage System]

Synonym for strip.

chunk size

CONTEXT [Storage System]

Synonym for stripe depth and strip size.

C-H-S addressing

CONTEXT [Storage System]

Synonym for cylinder-head-sector addressing.

CID

CONTEXT [iSCSI]

Acronym for Connection Identifier.

CIFS

CONTEXT [File System]

Acronym for Common Internet File System.

CIM
CONTEXT [Management] [Network]

Acronym for Common Information Model.

cipher
CONTEXT [Security]

Any cryptographic system in which arbitrary symbols or groups of symbols, represent units of plain text or in which units of plain text are rearranged, or both.

ciphertext
CONTEXT [Security]

Data that has been encrypted for security reasons. cf. cleartext

circuit
CONTEXT [Fibre Channel] [Network]

Synonym for communication circuit.

CKD (architecture)
CONTEXT [Storage System]

Synonym for count-key-data disk architecture.

Class 1
CONTEXT [Fibre Channel]

A connection-oriented class of communication service in which the entire bandwidth of the link between two ports is dedicated for communication between the ports and not used for other purposes. Also known as dedicated connection service. Class 1 service is not widely implemented. cf. intermix

Class 2
CONTEXT [Fibre Channel]

A connectionless Fibre Channel communication service which multiplexes frames from one or more N_Ports or NL_Ports. Class 2 frames are explicitly acknowledged by the receiver, and notification of delivery failure is provided. This class of service includes end to end flow control.

Class 3
CONTEXT [Fibre Channel]

A connectionless Fibre Channel communication service which multiplexes frames to or from one or more N_Portsor NL_Ports. Class 3 frames are datagrams, hat is they are not explicitly acknowledged, and delivery is on a "best effort" basis.

Class 4
CONTEXT [Fibre Channel]

A connection-oriented class of communication service in which a fraction of the bandwidth of the link between two ports is dedicated for communication between the ports. The remaining bandwidth may be used for other purposes. Class 4 service supports bounds on the maximum time to deliver a frame from sender to receiver. Also known as fractional service. Class 4 service is not widely implemented.

Class 6
CONTEXT [Fibre Channel]

A connection-oriented class of communication service between two Fibre Channel ports that provides dedicated unidirectional connections for reliable multicast. Also known as uni-directional dedicated connection service. Class 6 service is not widely implemented.

classified information
CONTEXT [Security]

Information that an appropriate agency has determined to require protection against unauthorized disclosure and has caused to be marked to indicate its classified status.

class of service

CONTEXT [Networking] [Fibre Channel]

1. A mechanism for managing traffic in a network by specifying message or packet priority.
2. The characteristics and guarantees of the transport layer of a Fibre Channel circuit. Fibre Channel classes of service include: connection services (Classes 1), guaranteed frame delivery with end to end flow control (Class 2), packetized frame datagrams (Class 3), quality of service sub-channels (e.g., constant sub rate or constant latency) (Class 4). Different classes of service may simultaneously exist in a fabric. The form and reliability of delivery in Class 3 circuits may vary with the topology. Different classes of service may simultaneously exist in a fabric.
3. The identification and grouping of data packets based on a priority label (in the packet header) or via other mechanisms (such as "per hop behavior", defined by the IETF's Differentiated Services).

cleartext

CONTEXT [Security]

Alternative term for plaintext. Data in clear text implies that the data is not scrambled or rearranged, and the data is in its raw form.

CLI

Acronym for command line interface.

client

1. An intelligent device or system that requests services from other intelligent devices, systems, or appliances. cf. server
2. An asymmetric relationship with a second party (a server) in which the client initiates requests and the server responds to those requests.

client service request

CONTEXT [Fibre Channel]

A request issued by a client application to a well-known service.
An example is a name service query.

cluster

A collection of computers that are interconnected (typically at high-speeds) for the purpose of improving reliability, availability, serviceability and/or performance (via load balancing). Often, clustered computers have access to a common pool of storage, and run special software to coordinate the component computers' activities.

CMIP

CONTEXT [Management] [Network]

Acronym for Common Management Information Protocol.

coaxial cable

An electrical transmission medium consisting of two concentric conductors separated by a dielectric material with the spacings and material arranged to give a specified electrical impedance. cf. triaxial cable

code balance

CONTEXT [Fibre Channel]

The number of 1 bits in a 10-bit transmitted data stream divided by 10 (e.g., 1110100011 has a code balance of 6/10 = 60%).

code bit

CONTEXT [Fibre Channel]

1.   A bit (binary digit) of an encoded datum. Sequences of code bits make up symbols, each of which corresponds to a data element (word, byte, or other unit).
2.   The smallest time period used by FC-0 for transmission on the media.

code byte

CONTEXT [Network]

A byte of an encoded datum. Sometimes called a symbol. Code bytes are the output of encoding or encryption processes. In communication theory contexts, a code byte is often referred to as a code word. cf. data byte

code violation

CONTEXT [Fibre Channel]

The error condition that occurs when a received transmission character cannot be decoded into a valid data byte or special code using the validity checking rules specified by the transmission code.

cold backup

CONTEXT [Data Recovery]

Synonym for offline backup. cf. hot backup , online backup

cold swap

The substitution of a replacement unit (RU) in a system for a defective one, where external power must be removed from the system in order to perform the substitution. A cold swap is a physical substitution as well as a functional one. cf. automatic swap, hot swap, warm swap

comma character

CONTEXT [Fibre Channel]

1. Either of the seven bit sequences 0011111 or 1100000 in an encoded stream
2. A special character containing a comma.

Command Descriptor Block

CONTEXT [SCSI]

A sequence of bytes that defines a single SCSI command sent to a SCSI target. Acronym CDB.

command line interface

A form of human interface to intelligent devices characterized by non-directive prompting and character string user input. Perceived by many users to be more difficult to comprehend and use than graphical user interfaces (GUI).

Common Criteria

CONTEXT [Security]

A multi-part International Standard that is meant to be used as the basis for evaluation of security properties of IT products and systems. The CC is specified in ISO/IEC 15408-1:1999, ISO/IEC 15408-2:1999, and ISO/IEC 15408-3:1999. Acronym CC.

Common Information Model

CONTEXT [Management] [Network]

An object oriented description of the entities and relationships in a business' management environment maintained by the Distributed Management Task Force. Abbreviated CIM. CIM is divided into a Core Model and Common Models. The Core Model addresses high-level concepts (such as systems and devices), as well as fundamental relationships (such as dependencies). The Common Models describe specific problem domains such as computer system, network, user or device management. The Common Models are subclasses of the Core Model and may also be subclasses of each other.

C

Common Internet File System

CONTEXT [Network]

A network file system access protocol primarily used by Windows clients to communicate file access requests to Windows servers. Abbreviated CIFS. Originally called Server Message Block (SMB). Today, other implementations of the CIFS protocol allow other clients and servers to use it for intercommunication and interoperation with Microsoft operating systems.Common Management Information Protocol

CONTEXT [Management] [Network]

A network management protocol built on the Open Systems Interconnection (OSI) communication model. Abbreviated CMIP. CMIP is more complete, and therefore larger than, SNMP.

communication circuit

CONTEXT [Fibre Channel] [Network]
1. A bidirectional path for message exchange within a Fibre Channel fabric.
2. In networking, a specific logical or physical path between two points over which communications occur.

communications security

CONTEXT [Network][Security]

Protection of information while it's being transmitted, particularly via telecommunications. A particular focus of cummunications security is message authenticity. Communications security may include cryptography, transmission security, emission security, and physical security.

complex array

CONTEXT [Storage System]

A disk array whose control software protects and maps data according to more complex algorithms than those of the Berkeley RAID Levels. The most common complex arrays are multi-level disk arrays, which perform more than one level of data address mapping, and adaptive arrays, which are capable of changing data address mapping dynamically.

compression

CONTEXT [Data Recovery] [File System] [Network] [Storage Device] [Storage System]

The process of encoding data to reduce its size. Lossy compression (i.e., compression using a technique in which a portion of the original information is lost) is acceptable for some forms of data (e.g., digital images) in some applications, but for most IT applications, lossless compression (i.e., compression using a technique that preserves the entire content of the original data, and from which the original data can be reconstructed exactly) is required.

computer security

CONTEXT [Security]

Measures and controls that ensure confidentiality, integrity, and availability of information system assets including hardware, software, firmware, and information being processed, stored, and communicated.

concatenation

CONTEXT [Network] [Storage System]

A logical joining of two series of data. Usually represented by the symbol "I". In data communications, two or more data are often concatenated to provide a unique name or reference (e.g., S_ID I X_ID). Volume managers concatenate disk address spaces to present a single larger address spaces.

concurrency

The property of overlapping in time. Usually refers to the execution of I/O operations or I/O requests.

concurrent

concurrent copy
CONTEXT [Storage System]

A hybrid point in time copy mechanism for which each copy is initially a changed block copy (i.e., shares unmodified storage with its source), but over time becomes a split mirror copy (i.e., does not share any storage with its source) without changing the point in time at which the copy logically occurred, independent of whether and where modifications to the source or the copy subsequently occur. A concurrent copy occupies at least the amount of storage required to hold changed blocks and grows to occupy as much storage as the copy source.

concurrent operations

Operations that overlap in time. The concept of concurrent I/O operations is central to the use of independent access arrays in throughput-intensive applications.

conditioning

The processing of a signal for the purpose of making it conform more closely to an ideal. Power conditioning is used to minimize voltage and frequency variations in an external power. Signal conditioning is used to reduce noise in logic or data signals.

confidentiality
CONTEXT [Security]

Encryption (in a security context).

configuration
CONTEXT [Storage System]

1. The process of installing or removing hardware or software components required for a system or subsystem to function.
2. Assignment of the operating parameters of a system, subsystem or device. Disk array configuration, for example, includes designating the array's member disks or extents, as well as parameters such as stripe depth, RAID model, cache allowance, etc.
3. The collection of a system's hardware and software components and operating parameters. cf. array configuration, physical configuration.

connection

CONTEXT [Fibre Channel] [iSCSI]

1. [Fibre Channel] Short form of dedicated connection.
2. [iSCSI] A communication path between the initiator and target using a TCP/IP connection. One or more connections make up a session. Connections carry control messages, SCSI commands, parameters, and data within iSCSI PDUs.

connection identifier

CONTEXT [iSCSI]

Each connection within a session has an identifier that is unique within the session. The initiator generates the ID and sends it to the target when logging in and out.

connection initiator

CONTEXT [Fibre Channel]

An N_Port which initiates a Class 1 connection with a destination N_Port through a connect-request and receives a valid response from the destination N_Port to establish the connection.

connection recipient

CONTEXT [Fibre Channel]

An N_Port which receives a Class 1 connect-request from a connection initiator and accepts the connection request by transmitting a valid response.

connectionless buffer

CONTEXT [Fibre Channel]

A receive buffer used in a connectionless service and capable of receiving connectionless frames.

connectionless frame

CONTEXT [Fibre Channel]

A frame used in a connectionless service (i.e., Class 1 frames with SOF(C1)., Class 2, and Class 3 frames referred to individually or collectively)

connectionless integrity service

CONTEXT [Security]

A security service that provides data integrity service for an individual IP datagram by detecting modification of the datagram without regard to the ordering of the datagram in a stream of datagrams.

connectionless service

CONTEXT [Fibre Channel]

Communication between two N_Ports or NL_Ports without a dedicated connection.

consistency group

CONTEXT [Storage System]

A collection of replication sets grouped together to ensure write order consistency across all the replication sets' primary volumes. An operation on a consistency group, such as changing replication from asynchronous to synchronous, applies to all the replication sets within the consistency group, and consequently their volumes.

console

1. A device for graphical or textual visual output from a computer system
2. In systems, network and device management, an application that provides graphical and textual feedback regarding operation and status, and that may accept operator commands and input influencing operation and status. Sometimes called enterprise management console.

consolidation

CONTEXT [Storage System]

The process of accumulating the data for a number of sequential write requests in a cache, and performing a smaller number of larger write requests to achieve more efficient device utilization.

C

Continuous Data Protection

CONTEXT [Data Recovery]

A data protection service that captures changes to data to a separate storage location. Acronym CDP. There are multiple methods for capturing the continuous changes involving different technologies that serve different needs. CDP-based solutions can provide fine granularities of restorable objects ranging from crash-consistent images to logical objects such as files, mail boxes, messages, etc.

continuously increasing relative offset

CONTEXT [Fibre Channel]

A transmission control algorithm in which the frames containing the subblocks that comprise a block of information are transmitted strictly in the order of the subblocks. Continuously increasing relative offset simplifies reassembly and detection of lost frames relative to random relative offset.

control software

CONTEXT [Storage System]

A body of software that provides common control and management for one or more disk arrays or tape arrays. Control software presents the arrays of disks or tapes it controls to its operating environment as one or more virtual disks or tapes. Control software may execute in a disk controller or intelligent host bus adapter, or in a host computer. When it executes in a disk controller or adapter, control software is often referred to as firmware.

controller

CONTEXT [Storage System] [Management]

1. The control logic in a disk or tape that performs command decoding and execution, host data transfer, serialization and deserialization of data, error detection and correction, and overall management of device operations
2. The control logic in a storage subsystem that performs command transformation and routing, aggregation (RAID, mirroring, striping, or other), high-level error recovery, and performance optimization for multiple storage devices
3. A subclass of CIM_LogicalDevice. A CIM_Controller represents a device having a single protocol stack whose primary purpose is to communicate with, control, and reset connected devices. There are many subclasses of CIM_Controller, addressing SCSI, PCI, USB, serial, parallel, and video controllers.

controller based array

controller based disk array

CONTEXT [Storage System]

A disk array whose control software executes in a disk subsystem controller. The member disks of a controller-based array are necessarily part of the same disk subsystem that includes the controller. cf. host based array.

controller cache

CONTEXT [Storage System]

A cache that resides within a controller and whose primary purpose is to improve disk or array I/O performance. cf. cache, disk cache, host cache.

COW

Acronym for copy on write.

copy on write

CONTEXT [Storage System] [Backup]

A technique for maintaining a point in time copy of a collection of data by copying only data which is modified after the instant of replicate initiation. The original source data is used to satisfy read requests for both the source data itself and for the unmodified portion of the point in time copy. cf. pointer remapping. Acronym COW.

copyback

CONTEXT [Storage System]

> The replacement of a properly functioning array member by another disk, including copying of the member's contents to the replacing disk. Copyback, which is most often used to create or restore a particular physical configuration for an array (e.g., a particular arrangement of array members on device I/O buses), is accomplished without reduction of the array.

count-key-data

CONTEXT [Storage Device]

> A disk data organization model in which the disk is assumed to consist of a fixed number of tracks, each having a maximum data capacity. Multiple records of varying length may be written on each track of a count-key-data disk, and the usable capacity of each track depends on the number of records written to it. Count-key-data (CKD) architecture derives its name from the record format, which consists of a field containing the number of bytes of data and a record address, an optional key field by which particular records can be easily recognized, and the data itself. Count-key-data is the storage architecture used by IBM Corporation's System 390 series of mainframe computer systems. cf. fixed block architecture.

countermeasure

CONTEXT [Security]

> Any action, device, procedure, technique, or other measure that reduces the vulnerability of or threat to a system.

covert channel

CONTEXT [Security]

> An unintended and/or unauthorized communications path that can be used to transfer information in a manner that violates a security policy.

credit

CONTEXT [Fibre Channel]

> The number of receive buffers allocated to a transmitting N_Port, NL_Port, or F_Port. The credit is the maximum number of outstanding frames that can be transmitted by that N_Port, NL_Port, or F_Port without causing a buffer overrun condition at the receiver.

CRC

Acronym for cyclic redundancy check.

CRL

CONTEXT [Security]

Acronym for Certificate Revocation List.

CRU

Acronym for Customer Replaceable Unit.

cryptanalysis

CONTEXT [Security]

A set of operations performed in converting encrypted information to plain text without initial knowledge of the algorithm and/or key employed in the encryption.

cryptography

CONTEXT [Security]

The principles, means and methods for rendering information unintelligible, and for restoring encrypted information to intelligible form.

cryptosystem

CONTEXT [Security]

A single means of encryption or decryption.

CSMA/CD

Acronym for Carrier Sense Multiple Access with Collision Detection.

cumulative incremental backup

CONTEXT [Data Recovery]

A backup in which all data objects modified since the last full backup are copied. To restore data when cumulative incremental backups are in use, only the latest full backup and the latest cumulative incremental backup are required. cf. differential incremental backup, full backup

current running disparity

CONTEXT [Fibre Channel]

The running disparity present at a transmitter when the encoding of a valid data byte or special code is initiated, or at a receiver when the decoding of a transmission character is initiated.

customer replaceable unit

A unit, or component of a system that is designed to be replaced by "customers;" i.e., individuals who may not be trained as computer system service personnel. cf. field replaccable unit

cut through (switching)

CONTEXT [Fibre Channel]

A switching technique that allows a routing decision to be made and acted upon as soon as the destination address of a frame is received.

cyclic redundancy check

A scheme for checking the correctness of data that has been transmitted or stored and retrieved. Abbreviated CRC. A CRC consists of a fixed number of bits computed as a function of the data to be protected, and appended to the data. When the data is read or received, the function is recomputed, and the result is compared to that appended to the data. Cyclic redundancy checks differ from error correcting codes in that they can detect a wide range of errors, but are not capable of correcting them. cf. error correcting code

cylinder-head-sector addressing

CONTEXT [Storage Device]

A form of addressing data stored on a disk in which the cylinder, head/platter combination, and relative sector number on a track are specified. Abbreviated C-H-S addressing. cf. block addressing

D_ID

CONTEXT [Fibre Channel]

Acronym for Destination Identifier. cf. S_ID

daemon

CONTEXT [Operating System]

A process that is always running on a computer system to service a particular set of requests. For example, in UNIX, lpd is a daemon that handles printing requests. Daemons are independent processes, and not part of an application program. Application requests may be serviced by a daemon.

DAS

Acronym for Direct Attached Storage.

data

The digital representation of anything in any form.

data availability

The amount of time that a data is accessible by applications during those time periods when it is expected to be available. Data availability is often measured as a percentage of an elapsed year. For example, 99.95% availability equates to 4.38 hours of unavailability in a year (0.0005 * 365 * 24 = 4.38) for a set of data that is expected to be available all the time. cf. availability, high availability

data byte

CONTEXT [Network] [Storage Device] [Storage System]

A byte of user data as presented to a storage or communication facility. Data bytes are input to processes that encode for transmission or encrypt for privacy. cf. code byte, data character.

data character

CONTEXT [Fibre Channel] [Network]

Any transmission character associated by the transmission code with a valid data byte.

Data classification

An organization of data into groups for management purposes. A purpose of a classification scheme is to associate service level objectives with groups of data based on their value to the business.

Data Encryption Standard

CONTEXT [Security]

A cryptographic data protection algorithm published by the National Institute of Standards and Technology in Federal Information Processing Standard (FIPS) Publication 46. Abbreviated DES. See also Triple DES.

data frame

CONTEXT [Fibre Channel]

A frame containing information meant for FC-4 (ULP) or the link application.

Data Lifecycle Management

CONTEXT [Information Lifecycle Management]

The policies, processes, practices, services and tools used to align the business value of data with the most appropriate and cost-effective storage infrastructure from the time data is created through its final disposition. Acronym DLM. Data is aligned with business requirements through management policies and service levels associated with performance, availability, recoverability, cost, etc. DLM is a subset of ILM.

data integrity

CONTEXT [Security]

The property that data has not been altered or destroyed in an unauthorized manner [ISO 7498-2:1988].

data management services
CONTEXT [Information Lifecycle Management]

> The control of data from the time it is created until it no longer exists. Data Management Services are not in the data path; rather, they provide control of, or utilize, data in the delivery of their services. This includes services such as data movement, data redundancy, and data deletion.

data manager
CONTEXT [File System]

D

> A computer program whose primary purpose is to present a convenient view of data to applications, and map that view to an internal representation on a system, subsystem or device. File systems and database management systems are the most common forms of a data manager.

data model

> A repository-specific representation of an information model. A database representation of the CIM schemas is an example of a data model..

data reliability

> Expressed as Mean Time to Data Loss (MTDL). The length of the stastically expected continuous span of time over which data stored by a population of identical disk subsystems can be correctly retrieved.

data replication
CONTEXT [Storage System]

> On an ongoing basis user data on a primary volume at the local site is copied to a secondary volume at a remote site for the purposes of providing high availability and redundancy of mission critical data. Data replication is also used for disaster recovery and business continuance.

Data shredding
CONTEXT [Information Lifecycle Management]

> A process for deleting data that is intended to make the data unrecoverable. For example, repeated overwrites of data on disk..

data stripe depth
CONTEXT [Storage System]

> Synonym for user data extent stripe depth.

data striping
CONTEXT [Storage System]

A disk array data mapping technique in which fixed-length sequences of virtual disk data addresses are mapped to sequences of member disk addresses in a regular rotating pattern. Disk striping is commonly called RAID Level 0 or RAID 0 because of its similarity to common RAID data mapping techniques. It includes no data protection, however, so strictly speaking, the appellation RAID is a misnomer.

data transfer capacity

The maximum rate at which data can be transmitted. Bandwidth is sometimes expressed in terms of signaling capacity (e.g., SCSI), and sometimes in terms of data transmission capacity inclusive of protocol overhead (e.g., Fibre Channel). cf. throughput, data transfer rate

data transfer-intensive (application)

A characterization of applications. A data transfer-intensive application is an I/O intensive application which makes large I/O requests. Data transfer-intensive applications' I/O requests are usually sequential.

data transfer rate

The amount of data per unit time actually moved across an I/O bus in the course of executing an I/O load. The data transfer capacity of an I/O subsystem is an upper bound on its data transfer rate for any I/O load. For disk subsystem I/O, data transfer rate is usually expressed in MBytes/second (millions of bytes per second, where 1 million = 10^6). cf. data transfer capacity

database management system
CONTEXT [Database]

An set of computer programs with a user and/or programming interface that supports the definition of the format of a database, and the creation of and access to its data. A database management system removes the need for a user or program to manage low level database storage. It also provides security for and assures the integrity of the data it contains. Types of database management systems are relational (table-oriented) and object oriented. Abbreviated DBMS.

datagram

CONTEXT [Fibre Channel] [Network]

A message sent between two communicating entities for which no explicit link level acknowledgement is expected. Datagrams are often said to be sent on a "best efforts" basis.

DBMS

CONTEXT [Database]

Acronym for database management system.

D

decoding

CONTEXT [Fibre Channel]

Validity checking of received transmission characters and generation of valid data bytes and special codes from those characters.

decryption

CONTEXT [Security]

The operations performed in converting encrypted information to plain text with full knowledge of the algorithm and key(s) used to encrypt it. Decryption is the intended method for an authorized user to decrypt encrypted information.

dedicated connection

CONTEXT [Fibre Channel]

A communication circuit between two N_Ports maintained by a Fibre Channel fabric. The port resources used by a dedicated connection cannot be used for other purposes during the life of the dedicated connection.

dedicated connection service

CONTEXT [Fibre Channel]

Synonym for Class 1 service.

degraded mode

CONTEXT [Storage System]

Synonym for reduced mode. A mode of RAID array operation in which not all of the array's member disks are functioning, but the array as a whole is able to respond to application read and write requests to its virtual disks.

degaussing
CONTEXT [Security]

A procedure that reduces magnetic flux to virtual zero by applying a reverse magnetizing field. Also called demagnetizing. Degaussing is used to ensure that no residual signal remains on magnetic media from which previously stored information could be recovered.

delimiter
CONTEXT [Fibre Channel]

An ordered set used to indicate a frame boundary.

delta snapshot
CONTEXT [Data Recovery]

An implementation of point in time copy that preserves the state of data at an instant in time without creating a full duplicate set of data.

DEN
CONTEXT [Network]

Acronym for Directory Enabled Network.

denial of service
CONTEXT [Security]

Result of any action or series of actions that prevents any part of an information system from functioning.

DES
CONTEXT [Security]

Acronym for Data Encryption Standard

Desktop Management Interface
CONTEXT [Management] [Network]

A former name for the Distributed Management Task Force (DMTF).

destination identifier
CONTEXT [Fibre Channel]

An address contained in a Fibre Channel frame that identifies the destination of the frame.

destination N_Port

CONTEXT [Fibre Channel]

The N_Port to which a frame is addressed.

device

CONTEXT [Management] [Storage System]

1. Synonym for storage device.
2. CIM_LogicalDevice is an object that abstracts the configuration and operational aspects of hardware. Subclasses of CIM_LogicalDevice include low-level sensors, processors, storage devices and printer hardware.

D

device bus

device I/O bus

CONTEXT [Storage System]

An I/O bus used to connect storage devices to a host bus adapter or intelligent controller. Device I/O bus is the preferred term.

device channel

CONTEXT [Storage System]

A channel used to connect storage devices to a host I/O bus adapter or intelligent controller. The preferred term is device I/O bus.

device fanout

CONTEXT [Storage System]

The ability of a storage controller to connect host computers to multiple storage devices using a single host I/O bus address. Device fanout allows computer systems to connect to substantially more storage devices than could be connected directly.

DH

CONTEXT [Security]

Acronym for Diffie-Hellman.

DH-CHAP

CONTEXT [Security]

Acronym for Diffie-Hellman augmented Challenge Handshake Authentication Protocol DH-CHAP is a password based Authentication and key management protocol that uses the CHAP algorithm (see RFC 1994) augmented with an optional Diffie-Hellmann algorithm. DH-CHAP provides bidirectional and may provide unidirectional Authentication between a Fibre Channel Initiator and Responder. DH-CHAP is defined by Fibre Channel – Security Protocols (FC-SP).

DHCP

CONTEXT [Network]

Acronym for dynamic host control protocol.

differential incremental backup

CONTEXT [Data Recovery]

A backup in which data objects modified since the last full backup or incremental backup are copied. To restore data when differential incremental backups are in use, the newest full backup and all differential backups newer than the newest full backup are required. cf. cumulative incremental backup, full backup

differential mirror resynchronization

differential resynchronization

CONTEXT [Data Recovery]

Synonyms for incremental mirror resynchronization.

differential (signaling)

CONTEXT [SCSI]

A SCSI electrical signaling technique in which each control and data signal is represented by a voltage differential between two signal lines. Differential signaling can be used over longer distances than the alternative single ended signaling. cf. single ended (signaling)

differentiated services

CONTEXT [Management]

A protocol defined by the IETF for managing network traffic based on the type of packet or message being transmitted. Abbreviated DiffServ. DiffServ rules define how a packet flows through a network based on a 6 bit field (the Differentiated Services Code Point) in the IP header. The Differentiated Services Code Point specifies the "per hop behavior" (bandwidth, queuing and forward/drop status) for the packet or message.

Diffie-Hellman

CONTEXT [Security]

A key agreement protocol (also called exponential key agreement) was developed by W. Diffie and M. E. Hellman in allowing two users to exchange a secret key over an insecure medium without any prior secrets. Acronym DH.

DiffServ

CONTEXT [Management]

Abbreviation for Differentiated Services.

digest

CONTEXT [Security]

A computationally efficient function mapping binary strings of arbitrary length to binary strings of some fixed length.

Digital Linear Tape

CONTEXT [Data Recovery]

A family of tape device and media technologies developed by Quantum Corporation.

digital signature

CONTEXT [Security]

A cryptographic process used to assure information authenticity, integrity, and nonrepudiation. Generally refers to assurances that can be externally verified by entities not in possession of the key used to sign the information. For example a secure hash of the information encrypted with the originator's private key when an asymmetric cryptosystem is used. Some algorithms that are used in digital signatures cannot be used to encrypt data. (e.g., DSA).

Digital Signature Algorithm
CONTEXT [Security]

A subset of the Digital Signature Standard that represents a specific public key algorithm that is only used for digital signatures. The secret key operates on the message hash generated by SHA-1; to verify a signature, one recomputes the hash of the message, uses the public key to decrypt the signature and then compares the results. Acronym DSA.

Digital Signature Standard
CONTEXT [Security]

A standard for digital signature that is published by the National Institute of Standards and Technology (NIST) in Federal Information Processing Standard (FIPS) Publication 186-2. It specifies DSA as the algorithm for digital signatures and SHA-1 for hashing. Acronym DSS.

Direct Attached Storage

Direct Attached Storage is a dedicated storage device that connects directly to one or more servers. Acronym DAS.

directory
CONTEXT [File System] [Management] [Network]
1. A mechanism for organizing information
2. A file or other persistent data structure in a file system that contains information about other files. Directories are usually organized hierarchically (i.e., a directory may contain both information about files and other directories), and are used to organize collections of files for application or human convenience.
3. An LDAP-based repository consisting of class definitions and instances of those classes. An example of an enterprise-wide LDAP directory is Microsoft's Active Directory (AD) or Novell's NetWare Directory Service (NDS).

directory enabled network
CONTEXT [Management] [Network]

An industry initiative, now part of the DMTF's mission, to map the CIM schema to an LDAP Directory. Abbreviated DEN. DEN's goals are to provide a consistent and standard data model to describe a network, its elements and its policies/rules. Policies are defined to provide quality of service or to manage to a specified class of service.

directory tree

CONTEXT [File System]

A collective term for a directory, all of its files, and the directory trees of each of its subdirectories.

Disaster Recovery

The recovery of data, access to data and associated processing through a comprehensive process of setting up a redundant site (equipment and work space) with recovery of operational data to continue business operations after a loss of use of all or part of a data center. This involves not only an essential set of data but also an essential set of all the hardware and software to continue processing of that data and business. This may involve some amount of down time to perform this recovery. Acronym DR.

discard policy

CONTEXT [Fibre Channel]

An error handling policy that allows an N_Port or NL_Port to discard data frames received following detection of a missing frame in a sequence.

disconnection

CONTEXT [Fibre Channel]

The process of removing a dedicated connection between two N_Ports.

disk

disk drive

CONTEXT [Storage Device]

A non-volatile, randomly addressable, re-writable data storage device. This definition includes both rotating magnetic and optical disks and solid-state disks, or non-volatile electronic storage elements. It does not include specialized devices such as write-once-read-many (WORM) optical disks, nor does it include so-called RAM disks implemented using software to control a dedicated portion of a host computer's volatile random access memory.

disk array
CONTEXT [Storage System]

> A set of disks from one or more commonly accessible disk subsystems, combined with a body of control software. The control software presents the disks' storage capacity to hosts as one or more virtual disks. Control software is often called firmware or microcode when it runs in a disk controller. Control software that runs in a host computer is usually called a volume manager.

disk array subsystem
CONTEXT [Storage System]

> A disk subsystem which includes control software with the capability to organize its disks as disk arrays.

disk block
CONTEXT [Storage Device] [Storage System]

> The unit in which data is stored and retrieved on a fixed block architecture disk. Disk blocks are of fixed usable size (with the most common being 512 bytes), and are usually numbered consecutively. Disk blocks are also the unit of on-disk protection against errors; whatever mechanism a disk employs to protect against data errors (e.g., ECC) protects individual blocks of data. cf. sector

disk cache

> 1. A cache that resides within a disk
> 2. A cache that resides in a controller or host whose primary purpose is to improve disk or array I/O performance. cf. cache, controller cache, host cache

disk image backup
CONTEXT [Data Recovery] [Windows]

> A backup consisting of a copy of each of the blocks comprising a disk's usable storage area. A disk image backup incorporates no information about the objects contained on the disk, and hence cannot be used for individual object restoration.

disk shadowing
CONTEXT [Storage System]

> Synonym for mirroring.

disk striping

CONTEXT [Storage System]

Synonym for data striping.

disk subsystem

CONTEXT [Storage System]

A storage subsystem that supports only disk devices.

disk scrubbing

CONTEXT [Storage System]

A function which reads all of the user data and check data blocks in a RAID array and relocates them if media defects are found. Disk scrubbing can have a noticeable negative effect on application performance.

disparity

CONTEXT [Fibre Channel]

The difference between the number of ones and the number of zeros in a transmission character.

Distributed Management Task Force

CONTEXT [Management]

An industry organization that develops management standards for computer system and enterprise environments. DMTF standards include WBEM, CIM, DMI, DEN and ARM. Abbreviated DMTF. The DMTF has a web site at www.dmtf.org.

DLM

CONTEXT [Information Lifecycle Management]

Acronym for Data Lifecycle Management.

DLT

CONTEXT [Storage Device]

Acronym for Digital Linear Tape.

DMI

Acronym for Desktop Management Interface.

DMR

Acronym for differential mirror resynchronization.

DMTF

CONTEXT [Management]

Acronym for Distributed Management Task Force.

DNS

CONTEXT [Network]

Acronym for Domain Name Service.

document type definition

CONTEXT [Network]

In XML, a specification of the permissible tags or "markup codes" in a document, and their meanings. Tags are delimited by the characters, "<" and ">". Abbreviated DTD. When a DTD is available for a document, a universal reader (program) can parse the document and display or print it.

DoD Trusted Computer System Evaluation Criteria

CONTEXT [Security]

A document published by the National Computer Security Center containing a uniform set of basic requirements and evaluation classes for assessing degrees of assurance in the effectiveness of hardware and software security controls built into systems. These criteria are intended for use in the design and evaluation of systems that will process and/or store sensitive or classified data. This document is Government Standard DoD 5200.28-STD and is frequently referred to as "The Orange Book" (because of its orange cover).

domain

1. A shared user authorization database which contains users, groups, and their security policies
2. set of interconnected network elements and addresses that are administered together and that may communicate.

domain controller

CONTEXT [Windows]

A Windows NT or Windows 2000 server that contains a copy of a user account database. A Windows domain may contain both a primary and a backup domain controller.

Domain Name Service

CONTEXT [Network]

A computer program that converts between IP addresses and symbolic names for nodes on a network in a standard way. Abbreviated DNS. Most operating systems include a version of Domain Name Service.

DoS

CONTEXT [Security]

Acronym for denial of service

D

double buffering

A technique often used to maximize data transfer rate by constantly keeping two I/O requests for consecutively addressed data outstanding. A software component begins a double-buffered I/O stream by making two I/O requests in rapid sequence. Thereafter, each time an I/O request completes, another is immediately made, leaving two outstanding. If a disk subsystem can process requests fast enough, double buffering allows data to be transferred at a disk or disk array's full volume transfer rate.

DR

Acronym for Disaster Recovery.

drive letter

CONTEXT [Windows]

A single letter of the alphabet by which applications and users identify a partition of physical or virtual disk to the Windows operating system. The number of letters in the alphabet limits the number of disks that can be referenced.

driver

driver software

Synonyms for I/O driver.

DSA

CONTEXT [Security]

Acronymfor digital signature algorithm.

DSS

CONTEXT [Security]

Acronym for Digital Signature Standard.

DTD

Acronym for Document Type definition.

dual active (components)

A pair of components, such as the controllers in a failure tolerant storage subsystem that share a task or class of tasks when both are functioning normally. When one of the components fails, the other takes on the entire task. Dual active controllers are connected to the same set of storage devices, improve both I/O performance and failure tolerance compared to a single controller. Dual active components are also called active-active components.

duplicate

CONTEXT [Data Recovery]

1. (noun) A general term for a copy of a collection of data, including point in time copies.
2. (verb) The action of making a duplicate as defined above. cf. replicate, snapshot
3. Any redundant component in a system.

Duplicate Removal

CONTEXT [Information Lifecycle Management]

The replacement of duplicate data with references to a shared copy in order to save storage space. This may be done at a whole-record level or at a sub-record level.

dynamic host control protocol

CONTEXT [Network]

An Internet protocol that allows nodes to dynamically acquire ("lease") network addresses for periods of time rather than having to pre-configure them. Abbreviated DHCP. DHCP greatly simplifies the administration of large networks, and networks in which nodes frequently join and depart.

dynamic mapping

CONTEXT [Storage System]

A form of mapping in which the correspondence between addresses in the two address spaces can change over time. cf. algorithmic mapping, tabular mapping

E_Port
CONTEXT [Fibre Channel]

> The "Expansion" port within a Fibre Channel switch connects to another Fibre Channel switch or bridge device via an inter-switch link. E_Ports are used to link Fibre Channel switches to form a multi-switch fabric.

EAL
CONTEXT [Security]

> Acronym for Evaluation Assurance Level.

EBU
CONTEXT [Standards]

> Acronym for European Broadcast Union.

ECC

> Acronym for error correcting code.

EE_buffer
CONTEXT [Fibre Channel]

> A buffer associated with end-to-end flow control.

EE_credit
CONTEXT [Fibre Channel]

> A credit scheme used to manage end-to-end flow control during the exchange of frames between two communicating devices.

electronic storage element
CONTEXT [Storage Device]

> Synonym for solid state disk.

embedded controller

embedded storage controller
CONTEXT [Storage System]

> An intelligent storage controller that mounts in a host computer's housing and attaches directly to a host's internal I/O bus. Embedded controllers obviate the need for host bus adapters and external host I/O buses. Embedded storage controllers differ from host bus adapters in that they provide functions beyond I/O bus protocol conversion (e.g., RAID).

Encapsulating Security Payload
CONTEXT [Security]

> A component of IPsec that permits the specification of various confidentiality mechanisms.

encoding
CONTEXT [Fibre Channel]

> Generation of transmission characters from valid data bytes and special codes.

encryption
CONTEXT [Security]

> The conversion of plaintext to encrypted text with the intent that it only be accessible to authorized users who have the appropriate decryption key.

end of frame

> A group of ordered sets that delineates the end of a frame.

end-to-end encryption

CONTEXT [Security]

> Encryption of information at its origin and decryption at its intended desti-
> nation without intermediate decryption.

end to end flow control

CONTEXT [Fibre Channel] [Network]

> 1. Control of message flow between the two end parties to a communi-
>   cation on a network
> 2. Flow control that occurs between two connected Fibre Channel N-Ports.

enterprise resource management

CONTEXT [Management] [Network]

> Software that manages all aspects of an organization's assets, systems,
> services and functions.
>
> The management of a set of resources in the wider perspective of an
> organization's entire business. Managing in an enterprise context
> requires that entities be named uniquely and locatable within the enterprise,
> that heterogeneity of platforms and services may be assumed, and that
> the dynamic nature of the environment is taken into account.

Enterprise Systems Connection

CONTEXT [Storage System]

> A 200 Mbps serial I/O bus used on IBM Corporation's Enterprise System
> 9000 data center computers. Abbreviated ESCON. Similar to Fibre Channel
> in many respects, ESCON is based on redundant switches to which com-
> puters and storage subsystems connect using serial optical connections.

entry port

exit port

CONTEXT [Data Recovery]

> A port in a media library through which media can be inserted or removed
> without exposing internal library components. Also called exit port.

EOF

> Acronym for end of frame.

ERM

Acronym for Enterprise Resource Management.

error correcting code

A scheme for checking the correctness of data that has been stored and retrieved, and correcting it if necessary. Abbreviated ECC. An ECC consists of a number of bits computed as a function of the data to be protected, and appended to the data. When the data and ECC are read, the function is recomputed, the result is compared to the ECC appended to the data, and correction is performed if necessary. Error correcting codes differ from cyclic redundancy checks in that the latter can detect errors, but are not generally capable of correcting them. cf. cyclic redundancy check

ESCON

CONTEXT [Storage System]

Acronym for Enterprise Systems Connection.

ESP

CONTEXT [Security]

Acronym for Encapsulating Security Payload

ESRM

Acronym for Enterprise Storage Resource Management.

Ethernet

CONTEXT [Network]

The predominant local area networking technology, based on packetized transmissions between physical ports over a variety of electrical and optical media. Ethernet can transport any of several upper layer protocols, the most popular of which is TCP/IP. Ethernet standards are maintained by the IEEE 802.3 committee.

The unqualified term Ethernet usually refers to 10 Mbps transmission on multi-point copper. Fast Ethernet is used to denote 100 Mbps transmission, also on multipoint copper facilities. Ethernet and Fast Ethernet both use CSMA/CD physical signaling. Gigabit Ethernet (abbreviated GBE) transmits at 1250 Megabaud (1Gbit of data per second) using 8b/10b encoding with constant transmission detection.

Ethernet adapter

CONTEXT [Network]

An adapter that connects an intelligent device to an Ethernet network. Usually called an Ethernet network interface card, or Ethernet NIC. cf. NIC

European Broadcast Union

CONTEXT [Standards]

A European-based television (Video) standardization group coordinated with SMPTE and loosely affiliated with FC-AV. Abbreviated EBU.

Evaluation Assurance Level

CONTEXT [Security]

An assurance package or a reusable set of assurance components that are combined together to satisfy a set of identified security objectives. The CC has provided seven predefined assurance packages, on a rising scale of assurance, which provide balanced groupings of the assurance components that are intended to be generally applicable. Acronym EAL.

EVSN

CONTEXT [Data Recovery]

Acronym for External Volume Serial Number.

exchange

CONTEXT [Fibre Channel]

A set of one or more non-concurrent related sequences passing between a pair of Fibre Channel ports. An exchange encapsulates a "conversation" such as a SCSI task or an IP exchange. Exchanges may be bidirectional and may be short or long lived. The parties to an exchange are identified by an Originator Exchange_Identifier (OX_ID) and a Responder Exchange_Identifier (RX_ID).

Exchange_Identifier

CONTEXT [Fibre Channel]

A generic term denoting either an Originator Exchange Identifier (OX_ID) or a Responder Exchange Identifier (RX_ID).

exchange status block

CONTEXT [Fibre Channel]

A data structure which contains the state of an exchange. An originator N_Port or NL_Port has an Originator Exchange Status Block and a Responder N_Port or NL_Port has a Responder Exchange Status Block for each concurrently active exchange.

exclusive connection

CONTEXT [Fibre Channel]

A Class 1 dedicated connection without intermix.

exit port

CONTEXT [Data Recovery]

A port in a media library through which media can be inserted or removed without exposing internal library components. cf. entry port

expansion card

expansion module

A collective term for optional adapters in the form of printed circuit modules that can be added to intelligent devices. Expansion cards include host bus adapters, network interface cards, as well as NVRAM, console, and other special purpose adapters.

expansion slot

A mounting and internal bus attachment device within an intelligent device into which expansion cards are inserted.

explicit addressing

CONTEXT [Storage Device] [Storage System]

A form of addressing used with disks in which the data's address is explicitly specified in the access request. cf. implicit addressing.

exploit

CONTEXT [Security]

A defined way to breach the security of an IT system through a vulnerability.

export (verb)

1. ynonym for present. To cause to appear or make available. Disk array control software exports virtual disks to its host environment. In file systems, a directory may be exported or made available for access by remote clients
2. To move objects, such as data, from within a system to a location outside the system, usually requiring a transformation during the move.

eXtensible Markup Language

A universal format for structured documents and data on the World Wide Web. Abbreviated XML. The World Wide Web Consortium is responsible for the XML specification. cf. http://www.w3.org/XML/.

E

extent

CONTEXT [Storage Device] [Storage System]

1. A set of consecutively addressed FBA disk blocks that is allocated to consecutive addresses of a single file
2. A set of consecutively located tracks on a CKD disk that is allocated to a single file.
3. A set of consecutively addressed disk blocks that is part of a single virtual disk-to-member disk array mapping. A single disk may be organized into multiple extents of different sizes, and may have multiple (possibly) non-adjacent extents that are part of the same virtual disk-to-member disk array mapping. This type of extent is sometimes called a logical disk.
4. A subclass or instance of the CIM_StorageExtent object. CIM models both removable and nonremovable types of storage media.

external controller

external disk controller

external storage controller

CONTEXT [Storage System]

An intelligent storage controller that mounts outside its host computer's enclosure and attaches to hosts via external I/O buses. External storage controllers usually mount in the enclosure containing the disks they control.

external volume serial number

CONTEXT [Data Recovery]

A humanly readable volume serial number on a removable media or cartridge. Abbreviated EVSN. . cf. label

eye

The region of an eye diagram that does not occur for correctly formed pulses. This is in the center of the eye diagram and distinguishes presence of signal (region above the eye) from absence of signal (region below the eye).

eye diagram

A diagram used to specify optical or electrical pulse characteristics for transmitters. The horizontal axis represents normalized time from pulse start and the vertical axis represents normalized amplitude. cf. eye opening

eye opening

The time interval across the eye, measured at a 50% normalized eye amplitude, which is error free to the specified BER.

F_Port

CONTEXT [Fibre Channel]

The "Fabric" port within a Fibre Channel fabric switch provides a point-to-point link attachment to a single N_Port. F_Ports are intermediate ports in virtual point-to-point links between end system ports, for example the N_Port on an end node to the F_Port on a switch to the F_Port in that switch to the N_Port on the other end node using a single Fibre Channel fabric switch.

F_Port name

CONTEXT [Fibre Channel]

A Name_Identifier associated with an F_Port.

fabric

CONTEXT [Fibre Channel]

An entity consisting of one or more Switches that interconnect various Nx_Ports attached to it. This entity is capable of routing frames using only the D_ID information in an FC-2 frame header.

fabric login

CONTEXT [Fibre Channel]

The process by which a Fibre Channel node establishes a logical connection to a fabric switch.

Fabric Name

CONTEXT [Fibre Channel]

A Name_Identifier associated with a fabric.

failback

The restoration of a failed system component's share of a load to a replacement component. For example, when a failed controller in a redundant configuration is replaced, the devices that were originally controlled by the failed controller are usually failed back to the replacement controller to restore the I/O balance, and to restore failure tolerance. Similarly, when a defective fan or power supply is replaced, its load, previously borne by a redundant component can be failed back to the replacement part.

failed over

A mode of operation for failure tolerant systems in which a component has failed and its function has been assumed by a redundant component. A system that protects against single failures operating in failed over mode is not failure tolerant, since failure of the redundant component may render the system unable to function. Some systems (e.g., clusters) are able to tolerate more than one failure; these remain failure tolerant until no redundant component is available to protect against further failures.

failover

The automatic substitution of a functionally equivalent system component for a failed one. The term failover is most often applied to intelligent controllers connected to the same storage devices and host computers. If one of the controllers fails, failover occurs, and the survivor takes over its I/O load.

failure tolerance

The ability of a system to continue to perform its function (possibly at a reduced performance level) when one or more of its components has failed. Failure tolerance in disk subsystems is often achieved by including redundant instances of components whose failure would make the system inoperable, coupled with facilities that allow the redundant components to assume the function of failed ones.

fanout

CONTEXT [Storage System]

Synonym for device fanout.

fast SCSI

CONTEXT [SCSI]

A form of SCSI that provides 10 megatransfers per second. Wide fast SCSI has a 16-bit data path, and transfers 20 MBytes per second. Narrow fast SCSI transfers 10 MBytes per second. cf. wide SCSI, Ultra SCSI, Ultra2 SCSI, Ultra3 SCSI.

fast mirror resynchronization

CONTEXT [Data Recovery]

A technique for reducing the time required to synchronize a split mirror with the set of storage devices from which it was split. Fast mirror resynchronization requires that a list of changes to the original set of data since moment of splitting be kept. When the split mirror is rejoined to the original set of volumes, only the data items identified in the list are copied from the original to the split mirror rather than the entire contents of the devices.

fault tolerance

Synonym for failure tolerance.

FBA

CONTEXT [Storage Device]

Acronym for Fixed Block Architecture.

FC-PH

CONTEXT [Fibre Channel]

The Fibre Channel physical standard, consisting of FC-0, FC-1, and FC-2.

FC-0

CONTEXT [Fibre Channel]

The Fibre Channel protocol level that encompasses the physical characteristics of the interface and data transmission media. Specified in FC-PH.

FC-1

CONTEXT [Fibre Channel]

The Fibre Channel protocol level that encompasses 8B/10B encoding, and transmission protocol. Specified in FC-PH.

FC-2

CONTEXT [Fibre Channel]

The Fibre Channel protocol level that encompasses signaling protocol rules and the organization of data into frames, sequences, and exchanges. Specified in FC-PH.

FC-3

CONTEXT [Fibre Channel]

The Fibre Channel protocol level that encompasses common services between FC-2 and FC-4. FC-3 contains no services in most implementations.

FC-4

CONTEXT [Fibre Channel]

The Fibre Channel protocol level that encompasses the mapping of upper layer protocols (ULP) such as IP and SCSI to lower protocol layers (FC-0 through FC-3). For example, the mapping of SCSI commands is an FC-4 ULP that defines the control interface between computers and storage.

FC-AE

CONTEXT [Fibre Channel]

Acronym for Fibre Channel Avionics Environment.

FC-AL

CONTEXT [Fibre Channel]

Acronym for Fibre Channel Arbitrated Loop.

FC-AV

CONTEXT [Fibre Channel]

Acronym for Fibre Channel Audio Video.

FC-GS2

CONTEXT [Fibre Channel]

Acronym for Fibre Channel Generic Services.

FC-SB

FC-SB2

CONTEXT [Fibre Channel]

Acronym for Fibre Channel Single Byte (command set).

FC-SW

FC-SW2

CONTEXT [Fibre Channel]

Acronym for Fibre Channel Switched (fabric interconnect).

FC-VI

CONTEXT [Fibre Channel]

Acronym for Fibre Channel Virtual Interface.

FCA

CONTEXT [Fibre Channel]

Acronym for Fibre Channel Association.

FCP

CONTEXT [Fibre Channel]

Acronym for Fibre Channel Protocol.

FCSI

CONTEXT [Fibre Channel]

Acronym for Fibre Channel Systems Initiative.

FDDI

CONTEXT [Network]

Acronym for Fiber Distributed Data Interface.

FIM

CONTEXT [Data Recovery]

Acronym for frozen image method.

FDDI adapter

CONTEXT [Network]

An adapter that connects an intelligent device to an FDDI network. Both FDDI-fiber adapters that connect to optical fiber FDDI networks, and FDDI-TP adapters that connect to twisted copper pair FDDI networks exist. Although network interface cards are usually referred to as NICs rather than as adapters, the term FDDI adapter is more common than FDDI NIC. cf. adapter, NIC

Federal Information Processing Standard

CONTEXT [Security]

Standards (and guidelines) produced by NIST for government-wide use in the specification and procurement of Federal computer systems.

Federated Management Architecture Specification

CONTEXT [Management] [Network]

A specification from Sun Microsystems Computer Corporation that defines a set of Java APIs for heterogeneous storage resource and storage network management. This specification is a central technology of Jiro.

Fiber Distributed Data Interface

CONTEXT [Network]

An ANSI standard for a token ring Metropolitan Area Networks (MANs), based on the use of optical fiber cable to transmit data at a rate of 100 Mbits/second. Both optical fiber and twisted copper pair variations of the FDDI physical standard exist. FDDI is a completely separate set of standards from Fibre Channel. The two are not directly interoperable.

fibre

CONTEXT [Fibre Channel]

1. A general term used to cover all transmission media specified in FC-PH
2. The X3T11 standardization committee's preferred spelling of the name of Fibre Channel technology.

Fibre Channel
CONTEXT [Fibre Channel]

A set of standards for a serial I/O bus capable of transferring data between two ports at up to 100 MBytes/second, with standards proposals to go to higher speeds. Fibre Channel supports point to point, arbitrated loop, and switched topologies. Fibre Channel was completely developed through industry cooperation, unlike SCSI, which was developed by a vendor and submitted for standardization after the fact.

Fibre Channel Association
CONTEXT [Fibre Channel]

A former trade association incorporated 1993 to promote Fibre Channel technology in the market. Abbreviated FCA. Separate FCA Europe and FCA Japan organizations also exist. In 1999, FCA merged with FCLC to form the FCIA.

F

Fibre Channel Avionics Environment
CONTEXT [Fibre Channel]

A technical committee and industry group whose goal is to standardize Fibre Channel for avionics, defense, and other mobile applications.

Fibre Channel Audio Video
CONTEXT [Fibre Channel]

defnition coming soon

Fibre Channel Arbitrated Loop
CONTEXT [Fibre Channel]

A form of Fibre Channel network in which up to 126 nodes are connected in a loop topology, with each node's L_Port transmitter connecting to the L_Port receiver of the node to its logical right. Nodes connected to a Fibre Channel Arbitrated Loop arbitrate for the single transmission that can occur on the loop at any instant using a Fibre Channel Arbitrated Loop protocol that is different from Fibre Channel switched and point to point protocols. An arbitrated loop may be private (no fabric connection) or public (attached to a fabric by an FL_Port).

Fibre Channel Community

Fibre Channel Loop Community

A former trade association incorporated 1995 to promote Fibre Channel Arbitrated Loop technology for storage applications. Abbreviated FCLC. Name changed to Fibre Channel Community in 1997 to reflect changing goals and interests of the organization. In 1999, FCLC merged with FCA to form the FCIA.

Fibre Channel Generic Services

CONTEXT [Fibre Channel]

An ANSI standard that specifies several Fibre Channel services such as the Name Server, Management Server, Time Server and others. Abbreviated FC-GS-2.

Fibre Channel Industry Association

CONTEXT [Fibre Channel]

The industry association resulting from the 1999 merger of the Fibre Channel Association and the Fibre Channel Community.

Fibre Channel Name

CONTEXT [Fibre Channel]

A Name_Identifier that is unique in the context of Fibre Channel. Essentially unused; most Fibre Channel name identifiers are World Wide Names that are unique across heterogeneous networks.

Fibre Channel Protocol

CONTEXT [Fibre Channel]

The serial SCSI command protocol used on Fibre Channel networks. Abbreviated FCP. FCP standardization is the responsibility of the X3T10 committee.

Fibre Channel Service Protocol

CONTEXT [Fibre Channel]

A FC-4 protocol that defines all services independently of topology or fabric type.

Fibre Channel Single Byte (command set)

CONTEXT [Fibre Channel]

> The industry standard command protocol for ESCON over Fibre Channel. Abbreviated FC-SB. A second version is known as FC-SB2.

Fibre Channel Switched (fabric interconnect)

CONTEXT [Fibre Channel]

> The standard governing the form of Fibre Channel network in which nodes are connected to a fabric topology implemented by one or more switches. Abbreviated FC-SW. Each FC-SW node's N_Port connects to an F_Port on a switch. Pairs of nodes connected to a FC-SW network can communicate concurrently. cf. fabric, Fibre Channel Arbitrated Loop

Fibre Channel Systems Initiative

CONTEXT [Fibre Channel]

> An industry association sponsored by Hewlett-Packard, IBM and SUN with the goals of creating Fibre Channel profiles and promoting use of Fibre Channel for computer systems applications. Abbreviated FCSI. FCSI was formed in 1993, and dissolved in 1995.

Fibre Channel Virtual Interface

CONTEXT [Fibre Channel]

> A proposed standard for application-level distributed interprocess communication based on Intel Corporation's V1.0 Virtual Interface (VI) Architecture; formerly known as VIA. Abbreviated FC-VI.

Fibre Connect

CONTEXT [Fibre Channel]

> IBM Corporation's implementation of ESCON over Fibre Channel. Abbreviated FICON. Later standardized as Fibre Channel Single Byte Command Set.

FICON

CONTEXT [Fibre Channel]

> Acronym for Fibre Connect.

field replaceable unit

A unit, or component of a system that is designed to be replaced "in the field;" i.e., without returning the system to a factory or repair depot. Field replaceable units may either be customer-replaceable, or their replacement may require trained service personnel. cf. customer replaceable unit

file

CONTEXT [File System]

An abstract data object made up of (a.) an ordered sequence of data bytes stored on a disk or tape, (b.) a symbolic name by which the object can be uniquely identified, and (c.) a set of properties, such as ownership and access permissions that allow the object to be managed by a file system or backup manager. Unlike the permanent address spaces of storage media, files may be created and deleted, and in most file systems, may expand or contract in size during their lifetimes.

file server

CONTEXT [File System]

A computer whose primary purpose is to serve files to clients. A file server may be a general purpose computer that is capable of hosting additional applications or a special purpose computer capable only of serving files. cf. filer

file system

CONTEXT [File System]

A software component that imposes structure on the address space of one or more physical or virtual disks so that applications may deal more conveniently with abstract named data objects of variable size (files). File systems are often supplied as operating system components, but are implemented and marketed as independent software comonents.

file system virtualization

1. The act of aggregating multiple file systems into one large virtual file system. Users access data objects through the virtual file system; they are unaware of the underlying partitioning.
2. The act of providing additional new or different functionality, e.g., a different file access protocol, on top of one or more existing file systems.

file virtualization

CONTEXT [File System]

1. The use of virtualization to present several underlying file or directory objects as one single composite file.
2. The use of virtualization to provide HSM like properties in a storage system.
3. The use of virtualization to present an integrated file interface when file data and metadata are managed separately in the storage system. cf. block virtualization

filer

CONTEXT [File System]

An intelligent network node whose hardware and software are designed to provide file services to client computers. Filers are pre-programmed by their vendors to provide file services, and are not normally user programmable. cf. appliance, file server

firmware

Low-level software for booting and operating an intelligent device. Firmware generally resides in read-only memory (ROM) on the device

fill byte

fill word

CONTEXT [Fibre Channel]

A transmission word that is an idle or an ARBx primitive signal. Fill words are transmitted between frames, primitive signals, and primitive sequences to keep a fibre channel network active.

FIPS

CONTEXT [Security]

Acronym for Federal Information Processing Standard.

fixed block architecture

A model of disks in which storage space is organized as linear, dense address spaces of blocks of a fixed size. Abbreviated FBA. Fixed block

Fixed Content

CONTEXT [Information Lifecycle Management]

Content that does not change.

FL_Port

CONTEXT [Fibre Channel]

A "Fabric Loop" port within a Fibre Channel fabric switch is capable of
Fibre Channel Arbitrated Loop operations and is connected to one or
more NL_Ports via a Fibre Channel Arbitrated Loop. An FL_Port becomes
a shared entry point for public NL_Port devices to a Fibre Channel fabric.
FL_Ports are intermediate ports in virtual point-to-point links between end
ports that do not reside on the same loop, for example the NL_Port on an
end node to the FL_Port on a switch to the F_Port in that switch to the
N_Port on that end node through a single Fibre Channel fabric switch.

FLOGI

CONTEXT [Fibre Channel]

Acronym for fabric login.

force break mirror

CONTEXT [Storage System]

Remove a mirror component from the mirror before the resilvering process
completes, causing the condition of its data to be Degraded. Just as
occurs with the break operation, the mirror component for which you
implement a force break becomes a standalone volume in the system;
however, it will not be accessible and should probably be deleted.

formatting

CONTEXT [Storage Device] [Storage System]

The preparation of a disk for use by writing required information on the
media. Disk controllers format disks by writing block header and trailer
information for every block on the disk. Host software components such
as volume managers and file systems format disks by writing the initial
structural information required for the volume or file system to be populated
with data and managed.

frame

CONTEXT [Fibre Channel]

An ordered vector of words that is the basic unit of data transmission in a
Fibre Channel network. A Fibre Channel frame consists of a Start of Frame
Word (SoF) (40 bits); a Frame Header (8 Words or 320 bits); data (0 to 524
Words or 0 to 2192 ten bit encoded bytes; a CRC (One Word or 40 bits);
and an End of Frame (EoF) (40 bits). cf. data frame

frame content
CONTEXT [Fibre Channel]

> The information contained in a frame between its Start-of-Frame and End-of-Frame delimiters, excluding the delimiters.

FRU

> Acronym for field Field Replaceable Unit.

FSP
CONTEXT [Fibre Channel]

> Acronym for Fibre Channel Service Protocol.

FMR
CONTEXT [Data Recovery]

> Acronym for fast mirror resynchronization..

full backup
CONTEXT [Data Recovery]

> A backup in which all of a defined set of data objects are copied, regardless of whether they have been modified since the last backup. A full backup is the basis from which incremental backups are taken. cf. cumulative incremental backup, differential incremental backup

full duplex

> Concurrent transmission and reception of data on a single link.

full volume transfer rate

> The average rate at which a single disk transfers a large amount of data (e.g., more than one cylinder) in response to one I/O request. The full-volume data transfer rate accounts for any delays (e.g., due to inter-sector gaps, inter-track switching time and seeks between adjacent cylinders) that may occur during the course of a large data transfer. Full volume transfer rate may differ depending on whether data is being read or written. If this is true, it is appropriate to speak of full-volume read rate or full-volume write rate. Also known as spiral data transfer rate.

frozen image
CONTEXT [Data Recovery]

> Synonym for point in time copy.

F

frozen image method

CONTEXT [Data Recovery]

A method by which a frozen image of a set of data can be generated. Abbreviated FIM. Split mirrors and copy-on-write snapshots are the two common methods of generating frozen images.

G_Port

CONTEXT [Fibre Channel]

A "Generic" Fabric Port can operate as either an E_Port or an F_Port. A G_Port can determine the operating mode at switch port initialization, F_Port when an N_Port attachment is determined, E_Port when an E_Port attachment is determined.

GBE

CONTEXT [Network]

Acronym for Gigabit Ethernet.

Gb

Gbit

gigabit

1. Shorthand for 1,000,000,000 (10^9) bits. Storage Networking Industry Association publications typically use the term Gbit to refer to 10^9 bits, rather than 1,073,741,824 (2^30) bits
2. For Fibre Channel, 1,062,500,000 bits per second

GB

GByte

Synonym for gigabyte. Shorthand for 1,000,000,000 (10^9) bytes. The Storage Networking Industry Association uses GByte to refer to 10^9 bytes, as is common in I/O-related applications rather than the 1,073,741,824 (2^30) convention sometimes used in describing computer system random access memory.

GBIC

CONTEXT [Fibre Channel]

Acronym for gigabit interface converter

geometry

The mathematical description of the layout of blocks on a disk. The primary aspects of a disk's geometry are the number of recording bands and the number of tracks and blocks per track in each, the number of data tracks per cylinder, and the number and layout of spare blocks reserved to compensate for media defects.

gigabaud link module

CONTEXT [Fibre Channel]

A transceiver that converts between electrical signals used by host bus adapters (and similar Fibre Channel devices) and either electrical or optical signals suitable for transmission. Abbreviated GLM. Gigabaud link modules allow designers to design one type of device and adapt it for either copper or optical applications. Gigabaud link modules are used less often than gigabit interface converters because they cannot be hot swapped. cf. gigabit interface converter

gigabit

Synonym for Gbit.

Gigabit Ethernet

CONTEXT [Network]

A group of Ethernet standards in which data is transmitted at 1Gbit per second. Gigabit Ethernet carries data at 1250 Megabaud using an adaptation of the Fibre Channel Physical Layer (8b/10b encoding); Abbreviated GBE. GBE standards are handled by IEEE 802.3z.

gigabit interface converter

CONTEXT [Fibre Channel]

A transceiver that converts between electrical signals used by host bus adapters (and similar Fibre Channel and Ethernet devices) and either electrical or optical signals suitable for transmission. Abbreviated GBIC. Gigabit interface converters allow designers to design one type of device and adapt it for either copper or optical applications. Unlike gigabaud link modules (GLMs), GBICs can be hot swapped, and are therefore gradually supplanting the former type of transceiver. cf. gigabaud link module

gigabyte

Synonym for GByte.

Gigabyte System Network

1. A common name for the HIPPI-6400 standard for 800 MByte per second links
2. A network of devices that implement the HIPPI-6400 standard.

GL_Port

CONTEXT [Fibre Channel]

A "Generic Loop" Fabric Port can operate as an E_Port, F_Port or FL_Port. A GL_Port can determine operating mode at switch port initialization, FL_Port when an NL_Port attachment is determined, F_Port when an N_Port attachment is determined, E_Port when an E_Port attachment is determined.

GLM

CONTEXT [Fibre Channel]

Acronym for gigabaud link module.

graphical user interface

A form of user interface to intelligent devices characterized by pictorial displays and highly structured, forms oriented input. Valued for perceived ease of use compared with character cell interface.

group

A collection of computer user identifiers used as a convenience in assigning resource access rights or operational privileges.

GSN

Acronym for Gigabyte System Network.

GUI

Acronym for Graphical User Interface.

hacker
CONTEXT [Security]

> An unauthorized user who attempts to gain and/or succeeds in gaining access to an information system.

hard zone
CONTEXT [Fibre Channel]

> A zone consisting of zone members which are permitted to communicate with one another via the fabric. Hard zones are enforced by fabric switches, which prohibit communication among members not in the same zone. well-known addresses are implicitly included in every zone.

Hashed Message Authentication Code
CONTEXT [Security]

> A value calculated over the contents of a message (usually using a cryptographic hash algorithm) that can be used to demonstrate that the contents of the message have not been changed during transmission. Acronym HMAC.

HBA

> Acronym for Host Bus Adapter.

hierarchical storage management

CONTEXT [Information Lifecycle Management]

The automated migration of data objects among storage devices, usually based on inactivity. Abbreviated HSM. Hierarchical storage management is based on the concept of a cost-performance storage hierarchy. By accepting lower access performance (higher access times), one can store objects less expensively. By automatically moving less frequently accessed objects to lower levels in the hierarchy, higher cost storage is freed for more active objects, and a better overall cost:performance ratio is achieved.

high availability

The ability of a system to perform its function continuously (without inter-ruption) for a significantly longer period of time than the reliabilities of its individual components would suggest. High availability is most often achieved through failure tolerance. High availability is not an easily quantifiable term. Both the bounds of a system that is called highly available and the degree to which its availability is extraordinary must be clearly understood on a case-by-case basis.

High Performance Parallel Interface

An ANSI standard for an 800 Mbit/second I/O interface primarily used in supercomputer networks. Abbreviated HIPPI. The subsequent 6400 Mbit per second I/O interface standard, HIPPI-6400, is more commonly referred to as the Gigabyte System Network (GSN) standard.

high speed serial direct connect

CONTEXT [Fibre Channel]

A form factor that allows quick connect/disconnect for Fibre Channel copper interfaces.

HIPPI

Acronym for High Performance Parallel Interface.

HMAC

CONTEXT [Security]

Acronym for Hashed Message Authentication Code.

host

A host computer.

host adapter

Synonym for host bus adapter.

host based array
host based disk array

CONTEXT [Storage System]

Synonym for volume. A disk array whose control software executes in one or more host computers rather than in a disk controller. The member disks of a host-based array may be part of different disk subsystems. cf. controller based array, volume.

host based virtualization

Virtualization implemented in a host computer rather than in a storage subsystem or storage appliance. Virtualization can be implemented either in host computers, in storage subsystems or storage appliances, or in a specific virtualization appliances in the storage interconnect fabric.

host bus

Synonym for host I/O bus.

host bus adapter

An I/O adapter that connects a host computer bus to a Fibre Channel or SCSI medium. Abbreviated HBA. Adapter is the preferred terms in Fibre Channel and SCSI contexts. The term NIC is used in networking contexts such as Ethernet and token ring.

host cache

CONTEXT [Storage]

A cache that resides within a host computer whose primary purpose is to improve disk or array I/O performance. Host cache may be associated with a file system or database, in which case, the data items stored in the cache are file or database entities. Alternatively, host cache may be associated with the device driver stack, in which case the cached data items are sequences of disk blocks. cf. cache, controller cache, disk cache

H

host computer

Any computer system to which disks, disk subsystems, or file servers are attached and accessible for data storage and I/O. Mainframes, servers, workstations and personal computers, as well as multiprocessors and clustered computer complexes, are all referred to as host computers in SNIA publications.

host environment

A storage subsystem's host computer or host computers, inclusive of operating system and other required software instance(s). The term host environment is used in preference to host computer to emphasize that multiple host computers are being discussed, or to emphasize the importance of the operating system or other software in the discussion.

host I/O bus

CONTEXT [Storage System]

An I/O bus used to connect a host computer's host bus adapter to storage subsystems or storage devices. cf. device I/O bus, I/O bus, channel

hot backup

CONTEXT [Data Recovery]

Synonym for online backup. cf. cold backup , offline backup

hot disk

A disk whose capacity to execute I/O requests is saturated by the aggregate I/O load directed to it from one or more applications.

hot file

A frequently accessed file. Hot files are generally the root cause of hot disks, although this is not always the case. A hot disk can also be caused by operating environment I/O, such as paging or swapping.

hot spare (disk)

A disk being used as a hot standby component.

hot standby (component, controller)

A redundant component in a failure tolerant storage subsystem that is powered and ready to operate, but which does not operate as long as a companion primary component is functioning. Hot standby components increase storage subsystem availability by allowing systems to continue to function when a component such as a controller fails. When the term hot standby is used to denote a disk, it specifically means a disk that is spinning and ready to be written to, for example, as the target of a rebuilding operation.

hot swap

The substitution of a replacement unit (RU) in a system for a defective unit, where the substitution can be performed while the system is performing its normal functioning normally. Hot swaps are physical operations typically performed by humans — cf. automatic swap, cold swap, warm swap.

hot swap adapter

An adapter that can be hot swapped into or out of an intelligent device. Some adapters that are called hot swap adapters should more properly be termed warm swap adapters, because the function they perform is interrupted while the substitution occurs.

HSM
CONTEXT [Data Recovery]

Acronym for hierarchical storage management.

HSSDC
CONTEXT [Fibre Channel]

Acronym for High Speed Serial Direct Connect.

HTML

Acronym for HyperText Markup Language.

HTTP

Acronym for HyperText Transfer Protocol.

hub

A communications infrastructure device to which nodes on a multi-point bus or loop are physically connected. Commonly used in Ethernet and Fibre Channel networks to improve the manageability of physical cables. Hubs maintain the logical loop topology of the network of which they are a part, while creating a "hub and spoke" physical star layout. Unlike switches, hubs do not aggregate bandwidth. Hubs typically support the addition or removal of nodes from the bus while it is operating.

hub port

CONTEXT [Fibre Channel]

A port on a Fibre Channel hub whose function is to pass data transmitted on the physical loop to the next port on the hub. Hub ports include loop healing port bypass functions. Some hubs have additional management functionality. There is no definition of a hub port in any Fibre Channel standard.

hunt group

CONTEXT [Fibre Channel]

A set of associated N_Ports in a single node attached to the same fabric. A hunt group is assigned a special alias address identifier that enables a switch to route any frames containing the identifier to be routed to any available N_Port in the group. FC-PH does not presently specify how a hunt group can be realized.

HyperText Markup Language

The set of tags or "markup" codes that describe how a document is displayed by a web browser. Tags are delimited by the characters, "<" and ">". For example, the markup code "<p>" indicates that a new paragraph is beginning, while "</p>" indicates that the current paragraph is ending.

HyperText Transfer Protocol

An application level protocol, usually run over TCP/IP, that enables the exchange of files via the World Wide Web.

I_T nexus

CONTEXT [SCSI]

According to SAM-2, the I_T nexus is a relationship between a SCSI Initiator Port and a SCSI Target Port.

ICMP

Acronym for Internet Control Message Protocol.

IDE

Acronym for Integrated Drive Electronics.

idempotency

A property of operations on data. An idempotent operation is one that has the same result no matter how many times it is performed on the same data. Writing a block of data to a disk is an idempotent operation, whereas writing a block of data to a tape is not, because writing a block of data twice to the same tape results in two adjacent copies of the block.

identification

CONTEXT [Security]

Process of determining the unique identity of an entity.

idle

idle word
CONTEXT [Fibre Channel]

> An ordered set of four transmission characters normally transmitted between frames to indicate that a fibre channel network is idle.

IDS
CONTEXT [Security]

> Acronym for intrusion detection system.

IETF
CONTEXT [Network] [Standards]

> Acronym for Internet Engineering Task Force.

iFCP
CONTEXT [Storage]

> iFCP is a gateway-to-gateway protocol, which provides fibre channel fabric services to fibre channel devices over a TCP/IP network.

ignored (field)
CONTEXT [Fibre Channel]

> A field that is not interpreted by its receiver.

IKE
CONTEXT [Network][Security]

> Acronym for Internet Key Exchange

ILM

> Acronym for Information Lifecycle Management.

implicit addressing
CONTEXT [Storage Device]

> A form of addressing usually used with tapes in which the data's address is inferred from the form of the the access request. Tape requests do not include an explicit block number, but instead specify the next or previous block from the current tape position, from which the block number must be inferred by device firmware. cf. explicit addressing

IMR

CONTEXT [Data Recovery]

Acronym for incremental mirror resynchronization.

in-band (transmission)

CONTEXT [Fibre Channel]

Transmission of a protocol other than the primary data protocol over the same medium as the primary data protocol. Management protocols are a common example of in-band transmission.

in-band virtualization

Virtualization functions or services that are in the data path. In a system that implements in-band virtualization, virtualization services such as address mapping are performed by the same functional components used to read or write data. cf. out-of-band virtualization

incremental backup

CONTEXT [Data Recovery]

Any backup in which only data objects modified since the time of some previous backup are copied. A collective term for cumulative incremental backups and differential incremental backups. cf. cumulative incremental backup, differential incremental backup , full backup.

incremental mirror resynchronization

incremental resynchronization

CONTEXT [Data Recovery]

A technique for reducing the time required to synchronize a split mirror with the set of storage devices from which it was split. Incremental mirror resynchronization requires that a list of changes to the original set of data since moment of splitting be kept. When the split mirror is rejoined to its original set of volumes, only the data items identified in the list are copied from the original to the split mirror (rather than the entire contents of the devices).

independent access array

A disk array whose data mapping is such that different member disks can execute multiple application I/O requests concurrently.cf. parallel access array

infinite buffer

CONTEXT [Fibre Channel]

A term indicating that at the FC-2 level, the amount of buffering available at the Sequence Recipient is assumed to be unlimited. Buffer overrun must be prevented by each ULP by choosing an appropriate amount of buffering per sequence based on its maximum transfer unit size.

information

CONTEXT [Information Lifecycle Management]

Information is data that is interpreted within a context such as an application or a process.

information category

CONTEXT [Fibre Channel]

A frame header field indicating the category to which the frame payload belongs (e.g., Solicited Data, Unsolicited Data, Solicited Control and Unsolicited Control).

Information Lifecycle Management

The policies, processes, practices, services and tools used to align the business value of information with the most appropriate and cost-effective infrastructure from the time information is created through its final disposition. Information is aligned with business requirements through management policies and service levels associated with applications, metadata and data. Acronym ILM.

information management services

CONTEXT [Information Lifecycle Management]

The processes associated with managing information as it progresses through various lifecycle states associated with a Business Process. These services exploit information about data content and relationships in making decisions, Examples include records management and content management applications.

information model

A repository-independent definition of entities (i.e., objects) and the relationships and interactions between these entities. For example, the CIM schemas are an example of an information model. An information model differs from a data model which is a repository-specific.

information system

CONTEXT [Security]

The entire infrastructure, organization, personnel and components for the collection, processing, storage, transmission, display, dissemination and disposition of information.

information technology

All aspects of information creation, access, use, storage, transport and management. The term information technology addresses all aspects of computer and storage systems, networks, users and software in an enterprise. Abbreviated IT.

information unit

CONTEXT [Fibre Channel]

An related collection of data specified by FC-4 to be transferred as a single FC-2 sequence.

infrastructure-based virtualization

Virtualization implemented in the storage fabric, in separate devices designed for the purpose, or in network devices. Examples are separate devices or additional functions in existing devices that aggregate multiple individual file system appliances or block storage subsystems into one such virtual service, functions providing transparent block or file system mirroring functions, or functions that provide new security or management services.

inherent cost

The cost of a system expressed in terms of the number and type of components it contains. The concept of inherent cost allows technology-based comparisons of disk subsystem alternatives by expressing cost in terms of number of disks, ports, modules, fans, power supplies, cabinets, etc. Because it is inexpensively reproducible, software is generally assumed to have negligible inherent cost.

initial relative offset

CONTEXT [Fibre Channel]

The relative offset of the block or sub-block transmitted by the first frame in a sequence. The initial relative offset is specified by an upper layer protocol and need not be zero.

initialization
CONTEXT [Fibre Channel]

1. The startup and initial configuration of a device, system, piece of software or network
2. For FC-1, the period beginning with power on and continuing until the transmitter and receiver at that level become operational.

initiator
The system component that originates an I/O command over an I/O bus or network. I/O adapters, network interface cards, and intelligent controller device I/O bus control ASICs are typical initiators. cf. LUN, originator, target, target ID.

Initiator Session Identifier
CONTEXT [iSCSI]

The unique identifier that an initiator assigns to its end point of the session. When combined with the iSCSI Initiator Name, it provides a worldwide unique name for its SCSI Initiator Port.

inode
CONTEXT [File System]

A persistent data structure in a UNIX or UNIX-like file system that describes the location of some or all of the disk blocks allocated to the file.

instantiation
The creation of an instance of a class or object oriented abstraction.

Integrated Drive Electronics
A type hardware interface widely used to connect hard disks, CD-ROMs and tape drives to a PC, but also used in other systems. The IDE interface is officially known as the ATA specification. Acronym IDE.

intelligent controller
CONTEXT [Storage System]

A storage controller that includes a processor or sequencer programmed to enable it to handle a substantial portion of I/O request processing autonomously.

intelligent device

A computer, storage controller, storage device, or appliance.

Intelligent Peripheral Interface

CONTEXT [Network]

A high-performance standards-based I/O interconnect. Abbreviated IPI.

intercabinet

CONTEXT [Fibre Channel]

A specification for Fibre Channel copper cabling that allows up to 30m distance between two enclosures that contain devices with Fibre Channel ports.

interconnect

A physical facility by which system elements are connected together and through which they can communicate with each other. I/O buses, and networks are both interconnects.

interface connector

CONTEXT [Fibre Channel]

An optical or electrical connector which connects the media to the Fibre Channel transmitter or receiver. An interface connector consists of both a receptacle and a plug.

intermix

CONTEXT [Fibre Channel]

A Fibre Channel class of service that provides a full bandwidth dedicated Class 1 connection, but allows connectionless Class 2 and Class 3 traffic to share the link during intervals when bandwidth is unused.

International Organization for Standardization

CONTEXT [Standards]

Worldwide federation of national standards bodies from more than 145 countries; short form of name is ISO. A non-governmental organization whose work results in international agreements that are published as International Standards and other types of ISO documents.

I

Internet Control Message Protocol

CONTEXT [Network]

A control protocol strongly related to IP and TCP, and used to convey a variety of control and error indications.

Internet Engineering Task Force

CONTEXT [Network][Security] [Standards]

A large open international community of network designers, operators, vendors, and researchers concerned with evolution and smooth operation of the Internet, and responsible for producing RFCs. The standards body responsible for Internet standards, including SNMP, TCP/IP and policy for QoS. Abbreviated IETF. The IETF has a web site at www.ietf.org.

Internet Key Exchange

CONTEXT [Network][Security]

A protocol used to obtain authenticated keying material. Standardized by the Internet Engineering Task Force and described in RFC 2409.

Internet Protocol

CONTEXT [Network]

A protocol that provides connectionless best effort delivery of datagrams across heterogeneous physical networks. Abbreviated IP. cf. TCP, UDP.

Internet Small Computer Systems Interface

CONTEXT [Storage]

A transport protocol that provides for the SCSI protocol to be carried over a TCP based IP network. Standardized by the Internet Engineering Task Force and described in RFC 3720. Acronym iSCSI.

Internet Storage Name Service

CONTEXT [iSCSI]

A protocol and mechanism for intelligent discovery of storage devices in an IP network. Acronym iSNS.

interrupt

A hardware or software signal that causes a computer to stop executing its instruction stream and switch to another stream. Software interrupts are triggered by application or other programs. Hardware interrupts are caused by external events, to notify software so it can deal with the events. The ticking of a clock, completion or reception of a transmission on an I/O bus or network, application attempts to execute invalid instructions or reference data for which they do not have access rights, and failure of some aspect of the computer hardware itself are all common causes of hardware interrupts.

interrupt switch

A human-activated switch present on some intelligent devices that is used to generate interrupts. Usually used for debugging purposes.

intracabinet

CONTEXT [Fibre Channel]

A Fibre Channel specification for copper cabling that allows up to 13m total cable length within a single enclosure that may contain multiple devices.

intrusion

CONTEXT [Security]

A deliberate or accidental set of events that potentially causes unauthorized access to, activity against, and/or activity in, an information technology (IT) system.

intrusion detection

CONTEXT [Security]

The process of identifying that an intrusion has been attempted, is occurring, or has occurred.

intrusion detection system

CONTEXT [Security]

A technical system that is used to identify and respond to intrusions in IT systems. Acronym IDS.

I/O

Acronym for input/output. The process of moving data between a computer system's main memory and an external device or interface such as a storage device, display, printer, or network connected to other computer systems. I/O is a collective term for reading, or moving data into a computer system's memory, and writing, or moving data from a computer system's memory to another location.

I/O adapter

1. An adapter that converts between the timing and protocol requirements of an intelligent device's memory bus and those of an I/O bus or network. In the context of storage subsystems, I/O adapters are contrasted with embedded storage controllers, which not only adapt between buses, but also perform transformations such as device fan-out, data caching, and RAID
2. Synonym for host bus adapter.

I/O bus

Any path used to transfer data and control information between components of an I/O subsystem. An I/O bus consists of wiring (either cable or backplane), connectors, and all associated electrical drivers, receivers, transducers, and other required electronic components. I/O buses are typically optimized for the transfer of data, and tend to support more restricted configurations than networks. In this book, an I/O bus that connects a host computer's host bus adapter to intelligent storage controllers or devices is called a host I/O bus. An I/O bus that connects storage controllers or host I/O bus adapters to devices is called a device I/O bus. cf. channel, device channel, device I/O bus, host I/O bus, network.

I/O bottleneck

Any resource in the I/O path (e.g., device driver, host bus adapter, I/O bus, intelligent controller, or disk) whose performance limits the performance of a storage subsystem as a whole.

I/O driver

A host computer software component (usually part of an operating system) whose function is to control the operation of peripheral controllers or adapters attached to the host computer. I/O drivers manage communication and data transfer between applications and I/O devices, using host bus adapters as agents. In some cases, drivers participate in data transfer, although this is rare with disk and tape drivers, since most host bus adapters and controllers contain specialized hardware to perform data transfers.

I/O intensity

A characterization of applications. An I/O-intensive application is one whose performance depends strongly on the performance of the I/O subsystem that provides its I/O services. I/O intensive applications may be data transfer intensive or I/O request intensive.

iSCSI Layer

Context [iSCSI]

The layer that builds/receives iSCSI PDUs and relays/receives them to/from one or more TCP connections that form an iSCSI session.

iSCSI Name

CONTEXT [iSCSI]

The name of an iSCSI initiator or iSCSI target.

iSCSI Network Entity

CONTEXT [iSCSI]

Represents a device or gateway that is accessible from the IP network. An iSCSI Network Entity has one or more iSCSI Network Portals.

iSCSI Network Portal

CONTEXT [iSCSI]

A component of an iSCSI Network Entity that has a TCP/IP address and can be used by a node within that entity for connections to another iSCSI node. An Initiator iSCSI Network Portal is identified by its IP address. A target iSCSI Network Portal is identified by its IP address and listening TCP port.

iSCSI Node

CONTEXT [iSCSI]

The iSCSI Node represents a single iSCSI initiator or iSCSI target.

iSCSI Portal Group

CONTEXT [iSCSI]

A set of iSCSI Network Portals within an iSCSI Node. When a session has multiple connections, all connections in a session must use the portals in a single iSCSI Portal Group.

iSCSI Portal Group Tag

CONTEXT [iSCSI]

Identifies an iSCSI Portal Group within an iSCSI Node. All portals in the group have the same iSCSI Portal Group Tag.

iSCSI Session

CONTEXT [iSCSI]

The top level relationship between a specific initiator and target, equivalent to the I_T nexus. A session can contain one or more connections.

iSCSI Session Identifier

CONTEXT [iSCSI]

Uniquely identifies a session between an iSCSI initiator and target.

iSCSI Target Name

CONTEXT [iSCSI]

Specifies the worldwide unique name of the iSCSI target..

iSCSI Target Node

CONTEXT [iSCSI]

Another name of the iSCSI target. An iSCSI Node within the iSCSI Server Network Entity.

iSCSI Target Port

CONTEXT [iSCSI]

Another name for a SCSI Target Port used for iSCSI.

ISID

CONTEXT [iSCSI]

Acronym for Initiator Session Identifier.

iSNS

CONTEXT [iSCSI]

Acronym for Internet Storage Name Service.

iSNS Discovery Domain

CONTEXT [iSNS]

Grouping of storage nodes for facilitating discovery and login control of these nodes.

ISO

CONTEXT [Standards]

Acronym for International Organization for Standardization.

IT

Acronym for Information Technology.

IT security

CONTEXT [Security]

As defined by ISO/IEC 1335 Information Technology – Guidelines for the management of IT Security, IT security comprises all aspects related to defining, achieving, and maintaining confidentiality, integrity, availability, non-repudiation, accountability, authenticity, and reliability of information assets.

I/O load

A sequence of I/O requests made to an I/O subsystem. The requests that comprise an I/O load include both user I/O and host overhead I/O, such as swapping, paging, and file system activity.

I/O load balancing

Synonym for load balancing.

I/O operation

A read, write, or control function performed to, from or within a computer system. For example I/O operations are requested by control software in order to satisfy application I/O requests made to virtual disks. cf. I/O request.

I/O request

A request by an application to read or write a specified amount of data. In the context of real and virtual disks, I/O requests specify the transfer of a number of blocks of data between consecutive disk block addresses and contiguous memory locations. cf. I/O operation.

I/O subsystem

CONTEXT [Storage System]

A collective term for the set of devices and software components that operate together to provide data transfer services. A storage subsystem is one type of I/O subsystem.

IP

CONTEXT [Network]

Acronym for Internet Protocol.

IPI

Acronym for Intelligent Peripheral Interface.

IPsec

CONTEXT [Network][Security]

Acronym for IP Security.

IP Security (IPsec)

CONTEXT [Network] [Security]

A suite of cryptographic algorithms, protocols and procedures used to protect information, authenticate communications, control access, and provide non-repudiation at the IP layer. The two key protocols are: the Authentication Header (AH) and Encapsulating Security Payload (ESP) protocols.

iSCSI

CONTEXT [Storage]

Acronym for Internet Small Computer Systems Interface.

iSCSI Device

CONTEXT [iSCSI]

A SCSI Device using an iSCSI service delivery subsystem. Service Delivery Subsystem is defined by SAM-2 as a transport mechanism for SCSI commands and responses.

iSCSI Initiator Name

CONTEXT [iSCSI]

Specifies the worldwide unique name of the initiator.

iSCSI Initiator Node

CONTEXT [iSCSI]

Another name for the iSCSI initiator. An iSCSI Node within the iSCSI Client Network Entity.

iSCSI Initiator Port

CONTEXT [iSCSI]

Another name for a SCSI Initiator Port used for iSCSI.

I

Java

An object oriented computer programming language that is similar to but simpler than C++. Java was created by Sun Microsystems Computer Corporation.

JBOD

CONTEXT [Storage Device] [Storage System]

Acronym for "Just a Bunch Of Disks." Originally used to mean a collection of disks without the coordinated control provided by control software; today the term JBOD most often refers to a cabinet of disks whether or not RAID functionality is present. cf. disk array

Jini

An architecture and supporting services for publishing and discovering devices and services on a network. Jini was created by Sun Microsystems Computer Corporation.

Jiro

A Sun Microsystems Computer Corporation initiative, developed using the Java Community Process. Jiro's goal is to enable the management of heterogeneous storage networks. The core technology in Jiro is defined in the Federated Management Architecture Specification.

jitter

CONTEXT [Fibre Channel]

> Deviation in timing that a bit stream encounters as it traverses a physical medium.

K28.5

CONTEXT [Fibre Channel]

A special 10-bit character used to indicate the beginning of a Fibre Channel command.

KB

KByte

Synonyms for kilobyte.

key

CONTEXT [Security]

Usually a sequence of random or pseudorandom bits used to direct cryptographic operations and/or for producing other keys. The same plaintext encrypted with different keys yields different ciphertexts, each of which requires a different key for decryption. In a symmetric cryptosystem the encryption and decryption keys are the same. In an asymmetric cryptosystem the encryption and decryption keys are different.

key backup

CONTEXT [Security]

A process used in a cryptographic system that can restore access to data by providing for key deposit and recovery. Key backup is sometimes used as replacement term for key escrow, which has become encumbered with additional meanings.

key escrow
CONTEXT [Security]

A process in which the storage of a cryptographic key is entrusted to a third party escrow agent who will disclose it only to the owner or another authorized user. Key escrow systems are used to ensure that access to encrypted data can be restored in case of key loss due to error, disaster or a malicious act.

key exchange
CONTEXT [Security]

A cryptographic protocol and procedure in which two communicating entities determine a shared key in a fashion such that a third party who reads all of their communication cannot effectively determine the value of the key. A common approach to key exchange requires such a third party to compute a discrete logarithm over a large field in order to determine the key value and relies on the computational intractability of the discrete logarithm problem for suitably selected large fields for its security.

key management
CONTEXT [Security]

The supervision and control of the process by which keys are generated, stored, protected, transferred, loaded, used, revoked and destroyed.

key pair
CONTEXT [Security]

A public key and its corresponding private key as used in public key cryptography (i.e., asymmetric cryptosystem).

key recovery
CONTEXT [Security]

A system characterized by the presence of some mechanism for obtaining exceptional access to a cryptographic key in case of loss by error, disaster, or malicious intent (see also key escrow).

keying material
CONTEXT [Security]

A key or authentication information in physical or magnetic form.

kilobyte

1.   1,000 (10^3) bytes of data. (Common storage industry usage)
2.   1,024 (2^10) bytes of data. (Common usage in software contexts).
Which is meant is typically clear from the context in which the term is used.

K

L_Port
CONTEXT [Fibre Channel]

> A "Loop" port is capable of performing arbitrated loop functions and protocols. NL_Ports and FL_Ports are examples of loop-capable ports.

label
CONTEXT [Data Recovery]

> An identifier associated with a removable media or cartridge. Labels may be humanly readable, machine readable, or both. cf. external volume serial number, media ID

LAN
CONTEXT [Network]

> Acronym for Local Area Network.

LANE
CONTEXT [Network]

> Acronym for Local Area Network Emulation.

LAN-free backup
CONTEXT [Data Recovery]

> A backup methodology that moves data over a SAN without using LAN resources. .

115

large read request

large write reques

large I/O request

An I/O request that specifies the transfer of a large amount of data. 'Large' obviously depends on the context, but typically refers to requests for 64 KBytes or more of cf. small I/O request

latency

1. Synonym for I/O request execution time, the time between the making of an I/O request and completion of the request's execution
2. Short for rotational latency, the time between the completion of a seek and the instant of arrival of the first block of data to be transferred at the disk's read/write head.

latent fault

A failure of a system component that has not been recognized because the failed aspect of the component has not been exercised since the occurrence of the failure. A field-developed media defect on a disk surface is a latent fault until an attempt is made to read the data in a block that spans the defect.

LBA

Acronym for logical block address.

LDAP

Acronym for Lightweight Directory Access Protocol.

LDM

Acronym for Logical Disk Manager.

LED

Acronym for Light Emitting Diode.

library

CONTEXT [Data Recovery]

A robotic media handler capable of storing multiple pieces of removable media and loading and unloading them from one or more drives in arbitrary order.

light emitting diode

A multimode light source based on inexpensive optical diodes. Abbreviated LED. Available in a variety of wavelengths; 1300 nanometer wavelength is typical for data communications. The practical transfer rate limit for LEDs is 266 Mbps.

Lightweight Directory Access Protocol

An IETF protocol for creating, accessing and removing objects and data from a directory. It provides the ability to search, compare, add, delete and modify directory objects, as well as modifying the names of these objects. It also supports bind, unbind and abandon (cancel) operations for a session. LDAP got its name from its goal of being a simpler form of DAP (Directory Access Protocol), from the X.500 set of standards.

link

CONTEXT [General] [Fibre Channel]

1. A physical connection (electrical or optical) between two nodes of a network.
2. [Fibre Channel] Two unidirectional fibres transmitting in opposite directions and their associated transmitters and receivers.
3. [Fibre Channel] The full-duplex FC-0 level association between FC-1 entities in directly attached ports.
4. [Fibre Channel] The point to point physical connection from one element of a Fibre Channel fabric to the next

LIP

CONTEXT [Fibre Channel]

Acronym for loop initialization primitive.

LISM

CONTEXT [Fibre Channel]

Acronym for loop initialization select master.

load balancing

The adjustment of system and/or application components and data so that application I/O or computational demands are spread as evenly as possible across a system's physical resources. I/O load balancing may be done manually (by a human) or automatically (by some means that does not require human intervention). cf. I/O load optimization, load sharing

L

load optimization

The manipulation of an I/O load in such a way that performance is optimal by some objective metric. Load optimization may be achieved by load balancing across several components, or by other means, such as request reordering or interleaved execution. cf. load balancing, load sharing

load sharing

The division of an I/O load or task among several storage subsystem components, without any attempt to equalize each component's share of the work. Each affected component bears a percentage of a shared load. When a storage subsystem is load sharing, it is possible for some of the sharing components to be operating at full capacity, to the point of actually limiting performance, while others are underutilized. cf. I/O load balancing, load optimization.

local area network

CONTEXT [Network]

A communications infrastructure designed to use dedicated wiring over a limited distance (typically a diameter of less than five kilometers) to connect a large number of intercommunicating nodes. Ethernet and token ring are the two most popular LAN technologies. cf. wide area network

local area network emulation

A collection of protocols and services that combine to create an emulated local area network using ATM as the underlying network. Abbreviated LANE. Local area network emulation enables intelligent devices with ATM connections to communicate with remote LAN-connected devices as if they were directly connected to the LAN.

local backup

CONTEXT [Data Recovery]

A backup methodology that utilizes host resources to copy data to a backup location that is under control of the same host.

local F_Port

CONTEXT [Fibre Channel]

The F_Port to which a particular N_Port is directly attached by a link.

logical block

CONTEXT [Storage Device] [Storage System]

A block of data stored on a disk or tape, and associated with an address for purposes of retrieval or overwriting. The term logical block is typically used to refer to the host's view of data addressing on a physical device. Within a storage device, there is often a further conversion between the logical blocks presented to hosts and the physical media locations at which the corresponding data is stored. cf. physical block, virtual block

logical block address

CONTEXT [Storage Device] [Storage System]

The address of a logical block. Logical block addresses are typically used in hosts' I/O commands. The SCSI disk command protocol, for example, uses logical block addresses.

logical disk

CONTEXT [Storage System]

A set of consecutively addressed FBA disk blocks that is part of a single virtual disk to physical disk mapping. Logical disks are used in some array implementations as constituents of logical volumes or partitions. Logical disks are normally not visible to the host environment, except during array configuration operations. cf. extent, virtual disk

logical disk manger

CONTEXT [Windows]

A name for the volume management control software in the Windows NT operating system.

logical unit

CONTEXT [SCSI]

L

The entity within a SCSI target that executes I/O commands. SCSI I/O commands are sent to a target and executed by a logical unit within that target. A SCSI physical disk typically has a single logical unit. Tape drives and array controllers may incorporate multiple logical units to which I/O commands can be addressed. Each logical unit exported by an array controller corresponds to a virtual disk. cf. LUN, target, target ID.

logical unit number

CONTEXT [SCSI]

The SCSI identifier of a logical unit within a target.

logical volume

CONTEXT [Storage System]

A virtual disk made up of logical disks. Also called a virtual disk, or volume set.

login server

CONTEXT [Fibre Channel]

An intelligent entity within a Fibre Channel fabric that receives and executes fabric login requests.

long wavelength laser

CONTEXT [Fibre Channel]

A laser with a wavelength 1300 nm or longer; usually 1300 or 1550 nanometers; widely used in the telecommunications industry.

loop initialization

CONTEXT [Fibre Channel]

The protocol by which a Fibre Channel Arbitrated Loop network initializes upon power up or recovers after a failure or other unexpected condition. Usually abbreviated LIP. During a LIP, the nodes present on the arbitrated loop identify themselves and acquire addresses on the loop for communication. No data can be transferred on an arbitrated loop until a LIP is complete.

loop initialization primitive

CONTEXT [Fibre Channel]

A Fiber Channel primitive used to (1.) initiate a procedure that results in unique addressing for all nodes, (2.) indicate a loop failure, or (3.) reset a specific node.

loop initialization select master

CONTEXT [Fibre Channel]

The process by which a temporary Fibre Channel arbitrated loop master is determined during loop initialization. Abbreviated LISM.

Loop Switch

Context [Fibre Channel]

A Fibre Channel switch operating at the layer 2 level allowing multiple dynamic point-to-point connections between devices using the FC-AL protocol. Loop switches do not implement the Fibre Channel Switch Fabric protocols (FC-SW-x standards).

loopback

CONTEXT [Fibre Channel]

An FC-1 operational mode in which information passed to the FC-1 transmitter is shunted directly to the FC-1 receiver. When a Fibre Channel interface is in loopback mode, the loopback signal overrides any external signal detected by the receiver.

loop port state machine

CONTEXT [Fibre Channel]

Logic that monitors and performs the tasks required for initialization and access to a Fibre Channel arbitrated loop.

LWL

CONTEXT [Fibre Channel]

Acronym for Long Wavelength Laser.

LUN

CONTEXT [SCSI]

Acronym for Logical Unit Number.

L

MAC

CONTEXT [Network] [Security]

1. [Network] Acronym for Media Access Control.
2. [Security] Acronym for Message Authentication Code.

magnetic remanance

CONTEXT [Security]

A magnetic representation of residual information remaining on a magnetic medium after the medium has been degaussed.

MAID

CONTEXT [Storage System]

Acronym for Massive Array of Idle Disks.

MAN

Acronym for Metropolitan Area Network.

Managed Object Format

CONTEXT [Management]

The syntax and formal description of the objects and associations in the CIM schemas. Abbreviated as MOF. MOF can also be translated to XML using a Document Type definition published by the DMTF.

Management Information Base

CONTEXT [Management]

The specification and formal description of a set of objects and variables that can be read and possibly written using the SNMP protocol. Abbreviated MIB. Various standard MIBs are defined by the IETF.

mandatory (provision)

CONTEXT [Standards]

A provision in a standard which must be supported in order for an implementation of the standard to be compliant.

mapping

CONTEXT [Storage System]

Conversion between two data addressing spaces. For example, mapping refers to the conversion between physical disk block addresses and the block addresses of the virtual disks presented to operating environments by control software.

mapping boundary

CONTEXT [Storage System]

A virtual disk block address of some significance to a disk array's mapping algorithms. The first and last blocks of a user data space strip or check data strip are mapping boundaries.

Massive Array of Idle Disks

CONTEXT [Storage System]

A storage system comprising an array of disk drives that are powered down individually or in groups when not required. Acronym MAID. MAID storage systems reduce the power consumed by a storage array.

maximum transfer unit

CONTEXT [Network]

The largest amount of data that it is permissible to transmit as one unit according to a protocol specification. Abbreviated MTU. The Ethernet MTU is 1536 eight bit bytes. The Fibre Channel MTU is 2112 eight bit bytes.

MB

MByte

Shorthand for megabyte.

Mb

Mbit

Shorthand for megabit.

MBps

Acronym for megabytes per second. A measure of bandwidth or data transfer rate.

Mbps

Acronym for megabits per second. A measure of bandwidth or data transfer rate.

MD5

CONTEXT [Security]

A specific message-digest algorithm producing a 128-bit digest which is used as authentication data by an authentication service.

mean time between failures

The average time from start of use to first failure in a large population of identical systems, components, or devices. Abbreviated MTBF.

mean time to (loss of) data availability

The average time from startup until a component failure causes a loss of timely user data access in a large population of storage devices. Loss of availability does not necessarily imply loss of data; for some classes of failures, (e.g., failure of non-redundant intelligent storage controllers, data remains intact, and can again be accessed after the failed component is replaced.

mean time to data loss

The average time from startup until a component failure causes a permanent loss of user data in a large population of storage devices. Mean time to data loss is similar to MTBF for disks and tapes, but is likely to differ in RAID arrays, where redundancy can protect against data loss due to component failures.

M

mean time to repair

The average time between a failure and completion of repair in a large population of identical systems, components, or devices. Mean time to repair comprises all elements of repair time, from the occurrence of the failure to restoration of complete functionality of the failed component. This includes time to notice and respond to the failure, time to repair or replace the failed component, and time to make the replaced component fully operational. In mirrored and RAID arrays, for example, the mean time to repair a disk failure includes the time required to reconstruct user data and check data from the failed disk on the replacement disk. Abbreviated MTTR.

meaningful (control field)

CONTEXT [Standards]

In a standard, a control field or bit that must be correctly interpreted by a receiver. Control fields are either meaningful or "not meaningful", in which case they must be ignored.

media

1.   The material in a storage device on which data is recorded.
2.   A physical link on which data is transmitted between two points.

media access control

CONTEXT [Network]

Algorithms that control access to physical media, especially in shared media networks.

media ID

CONTEXT [Data Recovery]

An machine readable identifier written on a piece of removable media that remains constant throughout the media's life. cf. external volume serial number, label

media manager

CONTEXT [Data Recovery]

A backup software component responsible for tracking the location, contents, and state of removable storage media. .

media robot
CONTEXT [Data Recovery]

Synonym for robotic media handler.

media stacker
CONTEXT [Data Recovery]

A robotic media handler in which media must be moved sequentially by the robot. Usually services a single drive. A stacker may be able to load media into a drive in arbitrary order, but must cycle through media in sequence to do so.

megabaud

One million baud (elements of transmitted information) per second, including data, signalling, overhead.

megabit

1,000,000 (10^6) bits. The SNIA uses the 10^6 convention commonly found in data transfer-related literature rather than the 1,048,576 (2^20) convention common in computer system random access memory and software literature.

megabyte

1,000,000 (10^6) bytes. The SNIA uses the 10^6 convention commonly found in storage and data transfer-related literature rather than the 1,048,576 (2^20) convention common in computer system random access memory and software literature.

megatransfer
CONTEXT [SCSI]

The transfer of one million data units per second. Used to describe the characteristics of parallel I/O buses like SCSI, for which the data transfer rate depends upon the amount of data transferred in each data cycle. cf. SCSI, fast SCSI, Ultra SCSI, Ultra2 SCSI, wide SCSI

member

member disk
CONTEXT [Storage System]

A disk that is in use as a member of a disk array.

message authentication code

CONTEXT [Security]

A cryptographic hash appended to a message to allow a receiver to ensure that the contents have not been changed in transit. Acronym MAC.

message-digest algorithm

CONTEXT [Security]

An algorithm which produces a secure hash.

metadata

CONTEXT [Information Lifecycle Management]

Data about other data. From ISO 14721.

metropolitan area network

CONTEXT [Network]

A network that connects nodes distributed over a metropolitan (city-wide) area as opposed to a local area (campus) or wide area (national or global). Abbreviated MAN. From a storage perspective, MANs are of interest because there are MANs over which block storageprotocols (e.g., ESCON, Fibre Channel) can be carried natively, whereas most WANs that extend beyond a single metropolitan area do not currently support such protocols.

MIB

CONTEXT [Management]

Acronym for Management Information Base.

MIME

CONTEXT [Network]

Acronym for Multipurpose Internet Mail Extensions.

mirror

CONTEXT [Storage System]

A storage volume consisting of separate components with identical contents that can be accessed independently by the Storage System.

mirror resynchronization
CONTEXT [Data Recovery]

The process of making the contents of a split mirror identical with the contents of the storage devices from which the mirror was split. Mirror resynchronization may entail copying the entire contents of the storage devices, or when fast mirror resynchronization is used, only the data items changed in the original since the instant of splitting.

mirroring
CONTEXT [Storage System]

A form of storage array in which two or more identical copies of data are maintained on separate media. Also known as RAID Level 1, disk shadowing, real-time copy, and t1 copy.

mirrors

mirrored disks
CONTEXT [Storage System]

The disks of a mirrored array.

mirrored array
CONTEXT [Storage System]

Common term for a disk array that implements RAID Level 1, or mirroring to protecting data against loss due to disk or device I/O bus failure.

MLS
CONTEXT [Security]

Acronym for multilevel security

modeling language

A language for describing the concepts of an information or data model. One of the most popular modeling languages in use today is UML (Unified Modeling Language). The essence of modeling languages is that they be capable of conveying the model concepts.

MOF
CONTEXT [Management]

Acronym for Managed Object Format.

monitor (program)

A program that executes in an operating environment and keeps track of system resource utilization. Monitors typically record CPU utilization, I/O request rates, data transfer rates, RAM utilization, and similar statistics. A monitor program, which may be an integral part of an operating system, a separate software product, or a part of a related component, such as a database management system, is a necessary prerequisite to manual I/O load balancing.

mount

In the Network File System (NFS), a protocol and set of procedures to specify a remote host and file system or directory to be accessed. Also specified is the location of the accessed directories in the local file hierarchy.

MTBF

Acronym for Mean Time Between Failures.

MTDA

Acronym for Mean Time until (Loss of) Data Availability.

MTDL

Acronym for Mean Time to Data Loss.

MTTR

Acronym for Mean Time To Repair.

MTU

CONTEXT [Network]

Acronym for Maximum Transfer Unit.

multicast

CONTEXT [Fibre Channel] [Network]

The simultaneous transmission of a message to a subset of more than one of the ports connected to a communication facility. In a Fibre Channel context, multi-cast specifically refers to the sending of a message to multiple N_Ports connected to a fabric.

multicast group

CONTEXT [Fibre Channel] [Network]

A set of ports associated with an address or identifier that serves as the destination for multicast packets or frames that are to be delivered to all ports in the set.

multi-level disk array

CONTEXT [Storage System]

A disk array with two levels of data mapping. The virtual disks created by one mapping level become the members of the second level. The most frequently encountered multi-level disk arrays use mirroring at the first level, and stripe data across the resulting mirrored arrays at the second level.

multilevel security

CONTEXT [Security]

Allows users and resources of different sensitivity levels to access a system concurrently, while ensuring that only information for which the user or resource has authorization is made available. Requires a formal computer security policy model which assigns specific access characteristics to both subjects and objects.

multimode (fiber optic cable)

CONTEXT [Fibre Channel] [Network]

A fiber optic cabling specification that allows up to 500 meter distances between devices.

multi-threaded

Having multiple concurrent or pseudo-concurrent execution sequences. Used to described processes in computer systems. Multi-threaded processes are one means by which I/O request-intensive applications can make maximum use of disk arrays to increase I/O performance.

M

multi-path I/O

CONTEXT [Storage System]

The facility for a host to direct I/O requests to a storage device on more than one access path. Multi-path I/O requires that devices be uniquely identifiable by some means other than by bus address.

Multipurpose Internet Mail Extensions

CONTEXT [Network]

A specification that defines the mechanisms for specifying and describing the format of Internet message bodies. An HTTP response containing a MIME Content-Type header allows the HTTP client to invoke the appropriate application for processing the received data.

mutual authentication

CONTEXT [Security]

A process that verifies the identity of both entities prior to establishing communication.

N_Port

CONTEXT [Fibre Channel]

A "Node" port connects via a point-to-point link to either a single N_Port or a single F_Port. . N_Ports handle creation, detection, and flow of message units to and from the connected systems. N_Ports are end ports in virtual point-to-point links through a fabric, for example the N_Port on an end node to F_Port on a switch to F_Port in that switch to the N_Port on the other end node using a single Fibre Channel fabric switch.

N_Port Name

CONTEXT [Fibre Channel]

A Name_Identifier associated with an N_Port.

NAA

CONTEXT [Network] [Standards]

Acronym for Network Address Authority.

Name_Identifier

CONTEXT [Fibre Channel]

A 64 bit identifier, consisting of a 60 bit value concatenated with a 4 bit Network_Address_Authority_Identifier. Name_Identifiers identify Fibre Channel entities such as N_Port, node, F_Port, or fabric.

133

name server
CONTEXT [Fibre Channel] [Network]

> An intelligent entity in a network that translates between symbolic node names and network addresses. In a Fibre Channel network, a name server translates between world wide names and fabric addresses.

naming

> The mapping of address space to a set of objects. Naming is typically used either for human convenience (e.g., symbolic names attached to files or storage devices), or to establish a level of independence between two system components (e.g., identification of files by inode names or identification of computers by IP addresses).

namespace
CONTEXT [File System] [Management]

> 1. The set of valid names recognized by a file system. One of the four basic functions of file systems is maintenance of a namespace so that invalid and duplicate names do not occur
> 2. In XML, a document at a specific Web address (URL) that lists the names of data elements and attributes that are used in other XML files
> 3. In CIM and WBEM, a collection of object definitions and instances that are logically consistent.

NAS
CONTEXT [Network] [Storage System]

> Acronym for network attached storage.

National Committee Information Technology Standards
CONTEXT [Standards]

> A committee of ANSI that serves as the governing body of X3T11 and other standards organizations.

National Institute of Standards and Technology
CONTEXT [Security]

> A non-regulatory federal agency within the U.S. Commerce Department's Technology Administration. NIST's mission is to develop and promote measurement, standards, and technology to enhance productivity, facilitate trade, and improve the quality of life. Specifically, the Computer Security Division within NIST's Information Technology Laboratory managed the Advanced Encryption Standard (AES) program.

NCITS
CONTEXT [Standards]

> Acronym for National Committee Information Technology Standards.

NDMP
CONTEXT [Management] [Network]

> Acronym for Network Data Management Protocol.

network
CONTEXT [Network]

> An interconnect that enables communication among a collection of attached nodes. A network consists of optical or electrical transmission media, infrastructure in the form of hubs and/or switches, and protocols that make message sequences meaningful. In comparison to I/O buses, networks are typically characterized by large numbers of nodes that act as peers, large inter-node separation, and flexible configurability. cf. channel, I/O bus, local area network, storage area network

network adapter
CONTEXT [Network]

> An adapter that connects an intelligent device to a network. Usually called a network interface card, or Ethernet NIC. cf. Ethernet adapter, NIC

Network Address Authority (NAA)
CONTEXT [Fibre Channel]

> NAA is a 4-bit field used to identify the controlling authority for guaranteeing uniqueness of WW Names. In a Fibre Channel environment, several Naming Authorities can be active at the same time, therefore Fibre Channel prepends the NAA field to World Wide Names to guarantee global uniqueness. An NAA =1, for example, indicates IEEE 48-bit Identifiers. The NAA also identifies one of several WWN formats, for example Format 1, Format 2 and Format 5.

N

network attached storage
CONTEXT [Network] [Storage System]

1. A term used to refer to storage elements that connect to a network and provide file access services to computer systems. Abbreviated NAS. A NAS Storage Element consists of an engine, which implements the file services, and one or more devices, on which data is stored. NAS elements may be attached to any type of network. When attached to SANs, NAS elements may be considered to be members of the SAS class of storage elements.

2. A class of systems that provide file services to host computers. A host system that uses network attached storage uses a file system device driver to access data using file access protocols such as NFS or CIFS. NAS systems interpret these commands and perform the internal file and device I/O operations necessary to execute them. cf. storage area network.

network backup
CONTEXT [Data Recovery]

A backup methodology that copies data over a LAN to a Backup Server.

Network Data Management Protocol
CONTEXT [Data Recovery]

A communications protocol that allows intelligent devices on which data is stored, robotic library devices, and backup applications to intercommunicate for the purpose of performing backups. Abbreviated NDMP.

An open standard protocol for network-based backup of NAS devices. Abbreviated NDMP. NDMP allows a network backup application to control the retrieval of data from, and backup of, a server without third-party software. The control and data transfer components of backup and restore are separated. NDMP is intended to support tape drives, but can be extended to address other devices and media in the future. The Network Data Management Task Force has a web site at http://www.ndmp.org.

Network File System (protocol)
CONTEXT [File System]

A distributed file system and its associated network protocol originally developed by Sun Microsystem Computer Corporation and commonly implemented in UNIX systems, although most other computer systems have implemented NFS clients and/or servers. Abbreviated NFS. The IETF is responsible for the NFS standard.

network interface card
CONTEXT [Network]

> An I/O adapter that connects a computer or other type of node to a network. Abbreviated NIC. A NIC is usually a circuit module, however, the term is sometimes used to denote an ASIC or set of ASICs on a computer system board that perform the network I/O adapter function. The term NIC is universally used in Ethernet and token ring contexts. In Fibre Channel contexts, the terms adapter and NIC are used in preference to host bus adapter. cf. adapter, host bus adapter, I/O adapter

NFS
CONTEXT [File System] [Storage System]

> Acronym for Network File System.

NIC
CONTEXT [Network]

> Acronym for Network Interface Card.

NIST
CONTEXT [Security]

> Acronym for National Institute of Standards and Technology

NL_Port
CONTEXT [Fibre Channel]

> A "Node Loop" port is capable of arbitrated loop functions and protocols. An NL_Port connects via an arbitrated loop to other NL_Ports and at most a single FL_Port. . NL_Ports handle creation, detection, and flow of message units to and from the connected systems. NL_Ports are end ports in virtual point-to-point links through a fabric, for example the NL_Port on an end node to FL_Port on a switch to the F_Port in that switch to the N_Port on the other end node using a single Fibre Channel fabric switch. In the absence of a fabric switch FL_Port, NL_Ports can communicate with other NL_Ports in virtual point-to-point links through a FC_AL open loop circuit often through FC_AL (Arbitrated Loop) hub or loop switch devices.

node
CONTEXT [Network] [Storage System]

> An addressable entity connected to an I/O bus or network. Used to refer to computers, storage devices, storage subsystems and network interconnection devices such as switches, routers and gateways. The component of a node that connects to the bus or network is a port.

N

node name

A Name_Identifier associated with a node.

Non-erasable Content

CONTEXT [Information Lifecycle Management]

Content that cannot be deleted in accordance with a retention policy.

normal operation

normal mode

A state of a system in which the system is functioning within its pre-scribed operational bounds. For example, when a disk array subsystem is operating in normal mode, all disks are up, no extraordinary actions (e.g., reconstruction) are being performed, and environmental conditions are within operational range. Sometimes called optimal mode.

non-linear mapping

CONTEXT [Storage System]

Any form of tabular mapping in which there is not a fixed size correspon-dence between the two mapped address spaces. Non-linear mapping is required in disk arrays that compress data, since the space required to store a given range of virtual blocks depends on the degree to which the contents of those blocks can be compressed, and therefore changes as block contents change. cf. algorithmic mapping, dynamic mapping, tabular mapping.

non-OFC (laser)

CONTEXT [Fibre Channel]

A laser transceiver whose lower-intensity output does not require special OFC mechanisms.

non-repeating ordered set

CONTEXT [Fibre Channel]

An ordered set passed by FC-2 to FC-1 for transmission which has non-idempotent semantics, i.e., it cannot be retransmitted.

nonrepudiation
CONTEXT [Security]

Assurance that a subject cannot later deny having performed some action. For communication, this may involve providing the sender of data with proof of delivery and the recipient with proof of the sender's identity, so neither can later deny having participated in the communication. Digital signatures are often used as a non-repudiation mechanism for stored information in combination with timestamps.

non-transparent failover

A failover from one component of a redundant system to another that is visible to the external environment. For example, a controller failover in a redundant disk subsystem is non-transparent if the surviving controller exports the other's virtual disks at different host I/O bus addresses or on a different host I/O bus. cf. transparent failover.

Non-Uniform Memory Architecture

A computer architecture that enables memory to be shared by multiple processors, with different processors having different access speeds to different parts of the memory. Abbreviated NUMA.

non-volatile random access memory

Computer system random access memory that has been made impervious to data loss due to power failure through the use of UPS, batteries, or implementation technology such as flash memory. Abbreviated NVRAM.

non-volatility

A property of data. Non-volatility refers to the property that data will be preserved, even if certain environmental conditions are not met. Used to describe data stored on disks or tapes. If electrical power to these devices is cut, data stored on them is nonetheless preserved.

not operational (receiver or transmitter)
CONTEXT [Fibre Channel]

A receiver or transmitter that is not capable of receiving or transmitting an encoded bit stream based on rules defined by FC-PH for error control. For example, FC-1 is not operational during initialization.

N

NUMA

Acronym for Non-Uniform Memory Architecture.

NVRAM

Acronym for Non-Volatile Random Access Memory.

NVRAM cache

A quantity of NVRAM used as a cache. NVRAM cache is particularly useful in RAID array subsystems, filers, database servers, and other intelligent devices that must keep track of the state of multi-step I/O operations even if power fails during the execution of the steps.

NVRAM card

A printed circuit module containing NVRAM.

object

CONTEXT [Security]

In the context of access control, an entity to which access is controlled and/or usage of which is restricted to authorized subjects. Information system resources are often examples of objects.

object oriented (methodology)

A methodology for decomposing an entity or problem by its key abstractions, versus by its procedures or steps. The key abstractions become classes in an information or data model, and embody well-defined behaviors called methods, with a unique set of data attributes. Instances of a class are called objects. Abbreviated OO.

OC-n

CONTEXT [Network]

A data rate that is a multiple of the fundamental SONET rate of 51.84 Mbits/sec. OC-3 (155 Mbits/sec), OC-12 (622 Mbits/sec), OC-48 (2488 Mbits/sec) and OC-192 (9953 Mbits/sec) are currently in common use. cf. Asynchronous Transfer Mode.

OFC

CONTEXT [Fibre Channel]

Acronym for Open Fibre Control.

offline backup

CONTEXT [Data Recovery]

> A form of backup in which the data being backed up is not accessed by applications for the duration of the backup.

online backup

CONTEXT [Data Recovery]

> A form of backup in which the data being backed up may be accessed by applications during the backup. Online backup of a set of data is usually accomplished through the use of a frozen image of the data.

OO

> Acronym for object oriented.

open

CONTEXT [General] [Fibre Channel]

> 1. [General] Any system or aspect of a system whose function is governed by a readily accessible standard rather than by a privately owned specification.
> 2. [Fibre Channel] A period of time that begins when a sequence or exchange is initiated and ends when the sequence or exchange is normally or abnormally terminated.
> 3. [General] Not electrically terminated, as an unplugged cable.

open fibre control

> A safety interlock system that limits the optical power level on an open optical fibre cable.

Open Group, the

> A cross-industry consortium for open systems standards and their certification. Unix, management and security standards are developed within the Open Group. The Open Group's web site is at www.opengroup.org.

open interconnect

> Synonym for standard interconnect.

operating environment

> A collective term for the hardware architecture and operating system of a computer system.

operation

CONTEXT [Fibre Channel]

An FC-2 construct that encapsulates one or more possibly concurrent exchanges into a single abstraction for higher level protocols.

Operation_Associator

CONTEXT [Fibre Channel]

A value used in the Association_Header to identify a specific operation within a node and correlate communicating processes related to that operation. The Operation_Associator is a handle by which an operation within a given node is referred to by another communicating Node. Operation_Associator is a generic reference to Originator Operation_Associator and Responder Operation_Associator.

operational (state)

CONTEXT [Fibre Channel]

The state of a receiver or transmitter that is capable of receiving or transmitting an encoded bit stream based on the rules defined by FC-PH for error control. Those receivers capable of accepting signals from transmitters requiring laser safety procedures are not considered operational after power on until a signal of a duration longer than that associated with laser safety procedures is present at the fibre attached to the receiver.

Operational Recovery

CONTEXT [Data Recovery]

Recovery of one or more applications and associated data to correct operational problems such as a corrupt database, user error or hardware failure. May use point in time copy or other techniques to create a consistent set of recoverable data. Acronym OR.

optical fall time

The time interval required for the falling edge of an optical pulse to transition between specified percentages of the signal amplitude. For lasers the transitions are measured between the 80% and 20% points. For LED media the specification points are 90% and 10%.

O

optional (characteristic)

CONTEXT [Standards]

Characteristics of a standard that are specified by the standard but not required for compliance. If an optional characteristic of a standard is implemented, it must be implemented as defined in in the standard.

OR

CONTEXT [Data Recovery]

Acronym for Operational Recovery.

ordered set

CONTEXT [Fibre Channel]

A transmission word (sequence of four 10-bit code bytes) with a special character in its first (leftmost) position and data characters in the remaining three positions. An ordered set is represented by the combination of special codes and data bytes which, when encoded, result in the generation of the transmission characters specified for the ordered set. Ordered sets are used for low-level Fibre Channel link functions such as frame demarcation, signaling between the ends of a link, initialization after power on, and some basic recovery actions.

originator

In a negotiation or exchange the party that initiates the negotiation or exchange.

Originator Exchange_Identifier

CONTEXT [Fibre Channel]

An identifier assigned by an originator to identify an exchange. Abbreviated OX_ID. An OX_ID is meaningful only to its originator.

overwrite procedure

CONTEXT [Security]

The process of writing patterns of data on top of the data stored on a magnetic medium for the purpose of obliterating the data.

out-of-band (transmission)

CONTEXT [Fibre Channel]

Transmission of management information for Fibre Channel components outside of the Fibre Channel network, typically over Ethernet.

out-of-band virtualization

Virtualization functions or services that are not in the data path. Examples are functions related to meta data, the management of data or storage, security management, backup of data, etc.

OX_ID

CONTEXT [Fibre Channel]

Acronym for Originator Exchange_Identifier.

0

panic

colloquial term describing a software program's reaction to an incomprehensible state. In an operating system context, a panic is usually a system call or unexpected state that causes the system to abruptly stop executing so as eliminate the possibility that the cause of the panic will cause further damage to the system, applications, or data.

parallel access array

CONTEXT [Storage System]

A disk array model in which data transfer and data protection algorithms assume that all member disks operate in unison, with each participating in the execution of every application I/O request. A parallel access array is only capable of executing one I/O request at a time. True parallel access would require that an array's disks be rotationally synchronized. In actual practice, arrays approximate parallel access behavior. Ideal RAID Level 2 and RAID Level 3 arrays are parallel access arrays. cf. independent access array

parallel (transmission)

Simultaneous transmission of multiple data bits over multiple physical lines.

parity disk

CONTEXT [Storage System]

In a RAID Level 3 or 4 array, the single disk on which the parity check data is stored.

147

parity RAID

CONTEXT [Storage System]

A collective term used to refer to Berkeley RAID Levels 3, 4, and 5.

parity RAID array

CONTEXT [Storage System]

A RAID array whose data protection mechanism is one of Berkeley RAID Levels 3, 4, or 5.

partition

CONTEXT [Storage System]

1. A subdivision of the capacity of a physical or virtual disk. Partitions are consecutively numbered ranges of blocks that are recognized by MS-DOS, Windows, and most UNIX operating systems.
2. Synonym for the type of extent used to configure arrays.
3. A contiguously addressed range of logical blocks on a physical media that is identifiable by an operating system via the partition's type and subtype fields. A partition's type and subtype fields are recorded on the physical media and hence make the partition self-identifying.

partitioning

CONTEXT [Storage System]

Presentation of the usable storage capacity of a disk or array to an operating environment in the form of several virtual disks whose aggregate capacity approximates that of the underlying physical or virtual disk. Partitioning is common in MS-DOS, Windows, and UNIX environments. Partitioning is useful with hosts which cannot support the full capacity of a large disk or array as one device. It can also be useful administratively, for example, to create hard subdivisions of a large virtual disk.

passive copper

CONTEXT [Fibre Channel]

A low-cost Fibre Channel connection that allows up to 13 meter copper cable lengths.

passphrase
CONTEXT [Security]

A sequence of characters longer than the acceptable length of a password that is transformed by a password system into a virtual password of acceptable length.

password
CONTEXT [Security]

A protected private alphanumeric string used to authenticate an identity or to authorize access to data.

path
1. The access path from a host computer to a storage device
2. The combination of device address and file system directory elements used to locate a file within a file system
3. Any route through an interconnect that allows two devices to communicate
4. A sequence of computer instructions that performs a given function, such as I/O request execution.

path length
CONTEXT [General] [Data Recovery] [File System]

1. [General] The number of instructions (a rough measure of the amount of time) required by a computer to perform a specific activity, such as I/O request execution.
2. [Data Recovery] [File System] The number of characters in a path name.

path name
CONTEXT [File System]

The complete list of nested sub-directories through which a file is reached.

payload
CONTEXT [Fibre Channel] [Network]

Contents of the data field of a communications frame or packet. In Fibre Channel, the payload excludes optional headers and fill bytes, if they are present.

PB

PByte

Acronym for petabyte (10^15 bytes).

PBC

CONTEXT [Fibre Channel]

Acronym for Port Bypass Circuit.

PCI

Acronym for Peripheral Component Interconnect.

pcnfsd

A daemon that permits personal computers to access file systems accessed through the NFS protocol.

PDC

CONTEXT [Windows]

Acronym for Primary Domain Controller.

PDU

CONTEXT [Network] [iSCSI]

Acronym for Protocol Data Unit.

peer

CONTEXT [Storage System]

In the context of data replication, one of two complimentary but physically separate systems. For example, user data is copied from a local system to a remote system; the remote system is considered the "peer" of the local system, and visa-versa.

penetration

CONTEXT [Security]

An unauthorized bypassing of the security mechanisms of a system.

Peripheral Component Interconnect

A bus for connecting interface modules to a computer system. Abbreviated PCI. Variations of PCI support 32 and 64 bit parallel data transfers at 33 and 66 MHz cycle times. A 133 MHz PCIX has been proposed by Compaq, HP, and IBM.

persistence

Synonym for non-volatility. Usually used to distinguish between data and metadata held in DRAM, which is lost when electrical power is lost, and data held on non-volatile storage (disk, tape, battery-backed DRAM, etc.) that survives, or persists across power outages.

petabyte

Shorthand for 1,000,000,000,000 (10^15) bytes. SNIA publications typically use the 10^12 convention commonly found in I/O literature rather than the 1,125,899,906,842,624 (2^50) convention sometimes used when discussing random access memory.

physical configuration

The installation, removal, or re-installation of disks, cables, HBAs, and other components required for a system or subsystem to function. Physical configuration is typically understood to include address assignments, such as PCI slot number, SCSI target ID and Logical Unit Number, etc. cf. array configuration, configuration.

physical block

CONTEXT [Storage Device]

A physical area on a recording media at which data is stored. Distinguished from the logical and virtual block views typically presented to the operating environment by storage devices.

physical block address

The address of a physical block. A number that can be algorithmically converted to a physical location on storage media.

physical disk

CONTEXT [Storage System] [Operating System]

1. [Storage System] A disk. Used to emphasize a contrast with virtual disks.
2. [Operating System] A host operating system's view of an online storage device.

physical extent

CONTEXT [Storage System]

A number of consecutively addressed blocks on a physical disk. Physical extents are created by control software as building blocks from which redundancy groups and volume sets are created. Called p_extent by ANSI.

physical extent block number

CONTEXT [Storage System]

The relative position of a block within a physical extent. Physical extent block numbers are used to develop higher-level constructs in RAID array striped data mapping, not for application or data addressing.

PKI

CONTEXT [Security]

Acronym for public key infrastructure

plaintext

CONTEXT [Security]

Unencrypted information.

PLDA

CONTEXT [Fibre Channel]

Acronym for Private Loop Direct Attach.

PLOGI

CONTEXT [Fibre Channel]

Acronym for port login.

point in time copy

CONTEXT [Data Recovery]

A fully usable copy of a defined collection of data that contains an image of the data as it appeared at a single point in time. The copy is considered to have logically occurred at that point in time, but implementations may perform part or all of the copy at other times (e.g., via database log replay or rollback) as long as the result is a consistent copy of the data as it appeared at that point in time. Implementations may restrict point in time copies to be read-only or may permit subsequent writes to the copy. Three important classes of point in time copies are split mirror, changed block, and concurrent. Pointer remapping and copy on write are implementation techniques often used for the latter two classes. cf. snapshot

pointer copy
CONTEXT [Data Recovery]

A point in time copy made using the pointer remapping technique.

pointer remapping
CONTEXT [Data Recovery]

A technique for maintaining a point in time copy in which pointers to all of the source data and copy data are maintained. When data is overwritten, a new location is chosen for the updated data, and the pointer for that data is remapped to point to it. If the copy is read-only, pointers to its data are never modified. cf. copy on write

policy (from RFC3198)
"Policy" can be defined from two perspectives:

Σ A definite goal, course or method of action to guide and determine present and future decisions. "Policies" are implemented or executed within a particular context (such as policies defined within a business unit).

Σ Policies as a set of rules to administer, manage, and control access to network resources [RFC3060].

Note that these two views are not contradictory since individual rules may be defined in support of business goals. (See also "policy goal", "policy abstraction" and "policy rule".)

policy goal (from RFC3198)
CONTEXT [Information Lifecycle Management]

Goals are the objectives or desired state intended to be maintained by a policy system. As the highest level of abstraction of policy, these goals are most directly described in business rather than technical terms. For example, a goal might state that a particular application operate on a network as though it had its own dedicated network, despite using a shared infrastructure. 'Policy goals' can include the objectives of a service level agreement, as well as the assignment of resources to applications or individuals. A policy system may be created that automatically strives to achieve a goal through feedback regarding whether the goal (such as a service level) is being met.

policy processor

In an intelligent device, the processor that schedules the overall activities. Policy processors are usually augmented by additional processors, state machines, or sequencers that perform the lower-level functions required to implement overall policy.

policy rule (from RFC3198)

CONTEXT [Information Lifecycle Management]

A basic building block of a policy-based system. It is the binding of a set of actions to a set of conditions - where the conditions are evaluated to determine whether the actions are performed [RFC3060].

port

A port can be an entrance to or exit from a storage network. It can be a connection point for a peripheral device or an application program. It can be logical, physical or both. Examples include Fibre Channel Port, Internet Protocol Suite Port and SCSI Port.

CONTEXT [Fibre Channel]

A Fibre Channel port provides physical interface attachment to other Fibre Channel ports. A Fibre Channel port includes the transmitter, receiver and associated logic at either end of a link within a Node. There may be multiple Ports per Node. Each Port is assigned a unique Port_ID, which is the Fibre Channel address used for routing. Each port is identified by a unique World Wide Port Name (WW Port Name) Ports can be implemented on Host Bus Adapters (HBAs), Storage Adapters (SAs), routers, switches, bridges, gateways, etc.

Fibre Channel ports may have many different logical operating modes, such as N_Port, NL_Port, F_Port, FL_Port, E_Port and B_Port. Fibre Channel Services are accessed using Fibre Channel Well-Known addresses, for example the Directory/Name Server at x'FFFFFC' and the Fabric Port Login Server at x'FFFFFD'. These are accessed and addressed as other ports and can also be considered logical.

P

Ethernet uses Media Access Control identifiers (commonly referred to as MAC addresses) to distinguish between separate logical channels connecting two ports on the same physical transport network interface.

The Transmission Control Protocol (TCP) and the User Datagram Protocol (UDP) of the Internet Protocol Suite use logical ports as communication endpoints, including client-side user ports (source of application requests) and server-side well-known ports for service access. Examples of well-known server-side ports include:

- Internet Small Computer Systems Interface (iSCSI – 3260)
- File Transfer Protocol (FTP Data – 20, FTP Control – 21)
- Simple Mail Transfer Protocol (SMTP – 25)
- Hypertext Transfer Protocol (HTTP – 80)
- Network File System (NFS - 2049)

CONTEXT [SCSI]

A SCSI Bus physical port provides a means that allows a device to connect the drivers and receivers to the SCSI parallel bus cable.

A SCSI logical port is either a SCSI initiator port or a SCSI target port; it is the logical entity that originates or processes SCSI commands (including data transfer) and task management requests. For example, the SCSI initiator port enables SCSI operations to flow to and from a server operating system device driver. The SCSI target port enables access to a LUN giving access to a disc drive or access to a range of LUNs configured and implemented through the physical target port on a storage controller.

Port_ID

CONTEXT [Fibre Channel]

A unique 24 bit address used for frame routing and assigned to an N_Port or NL_Port. The Port_ID hierarchic includes an 8-bit Domain ID (typically a switch number), an 8-bit Area ID (a port or group of switch ports) and an 8-bit Device ID (typically 00 for N_Ports or for NL_Ports, the Loop Initialization assigned Arbitrated Loop Physical Address (ALPA). The Port_ID of the Source, Port (S_ID) and the Port_ID of the Destination Port, (D_ID) is used in the Fibre Channel frame header for routing.

port bypass circuit
CONTEXT [Fibre Channel]

> A circuit that automatically opens and closes a Fibre Channel arbitrated loop so that nodes can be added to or removed from the loop with minimal disruption of operations. Port bypass circuits are typically found in Fibre Channel hubs and disk enclosures.

port login
CONTEXT [Fibre Channel]

> The port-to-port login process by which Fibre Channel initiators establish sessions with targets.

port name
CONTEXT [Fibre Channel]

> A unique 64-bit indentifier assigned to a Fibre Channel port.

POST

> Acronym for Power On Self Test.

power conditioning

> The regulation of power supplied to a system so that acceptable ranges of voltage and frequency are maintained. Power conditioning is sometimes done by a storage subsystem, but may also be an environmental requirement.

power on self test

> A set of internally stored diagnostic programs run by intelligent devices when powered on. Abbreviated POST. These diagnostic programs verify the basic integrity of hardware before software is permitted to run on it.

PP
CONTEXT [Security]

> Acronym for protection profile.

present (verb)

> To cause to appear or to make available. For example, RAID control software and volume managers present virtual disks to host environments. Synonym for export.

primary domain controller

CONTEXT [Windows]

A domain controller that has been assigned as or has negotiated to become the primary authentication server for the domain of which it is a part.

primitive sequence

CONTEXT [Fibre Channel]

An ordered set transmitted repeatedly and continuously until a specified response is received.

primitive signal

CONTEXT [Fibre Channel]

An ordered set with a special meaning such as an idle or Receiver_Ready (R_RDY).

private key

CONTEXT [Security]

A key which is used in a symmetric cryptosystem in both encryption and decryption processes, or in an asymmetric cryptosystem for one, but not both, of those processes. A private key must remain confidential to the using party if communication security is to be maintained.

private key cryptography

CONTEXT [Security]

An encryption methodology in which the encryptor and decryptor use the same key, which must be kept secret. cf. symmetric cryptosystem.

private loop

CONTEXT [Fibre Channel]

A Fibre Channel arbitrated loop with no fabric attachment.

private loop device

CONTEXT [Fibre Channel]

A Fibre Channel arbitrated loop device that does not support fabric login.

process policy

CONTEXT [Fibre Channel]

An error handling policy that allows an N_Port to continue processing data frames following detection of one or more missing frames in a sequence.

Process_Associator

CONTEXT [Fibre Channel]

A value in the Association_Header that identifies a process or a group of processes within a node. Communicating processes in different nodes use Process_Associators to address each other. Originating processes have Originator Process_Associators; responding processes have Responder Process_Associators.

profile

CONTEXT [Standards]

A proper subset of a standard that supports interoperability across a set of products or in a specific application. Profiles exist for FCP (FCSI and PLDA), IP, and other areas. A profile is a vertical slice through a standard containing physical, logical and behavioral elements required for interoperability.

proprietary interconnect

proprietary I/O bus

CONTEXT [Storage System]

An I/O bus (either a host I/O bus or a device I/O bus) whose transmission characteristics and protocols are the intellectual property of a single vendor, and which require the permission of that vendor to be implemented in the products of other vendors. cf. open interconnect.

protected space

protected space extent

The storage space available for application data in a physical extent that belongs to a redundancy group.

Protection Profile

CONTEXT [Security]

An implementation-independent set of security functional and assurance requirements for a category of IT products that meet specific consumer needs. It is most commonly associated with ISO 15408. Acronym PP.

protocol

CONTEXT [Fibre Channel] [Network] [SCSI]

A set of rules for using an interconnect or network so that information conveyed on the interconnect can be correctly interpreted by all parties to the communication. Protocols include such aspects of communication as data representation, data item ordering, message formats, message and response sequencing rules, block data transmission conventions, timing requirements, and so forth.

Protocol Data Unit

CONTEXT [Network] [iSCSI]

1. [Network] A single message between two network nodes used for communication.
2. [iSCSI] The term used to describe one iSCSI message sent by either a target or an initiator in an iSCSI connection.

public key

CONTEXT [Security]

A key which is used in an asymmetric cryptosystem for either the encryption or decryption process where the private key is not used, and which can be shared amongst a group of users without impacting the security of the cryptosystem.

public key cryptography

CONTEXT [Security]

An encryption system using a linked pair of keys. What one key of the pair encrypts, the other decrypts. Either key can be used for encryption and decryption. See also asymmetric cryptosystem.

Public Key Infrastructure

CONTEXT [Security]

A collection of software, hardware, people and procedures that facilitate secure creation and management of digital certificates.

public loop

CONTEXT [Fibre Channel]

A Fibre Channel arbitrated loop with an attachment to a fabric.

public loop device

CONTEXT [Fibre Channel]

A Fibre Channel arbitrated loop device that supports fabric login and services.

pull technology

The transmission of information in response to a request for that information. An example of a pull technology is polling. cf. push technology.

push technology

The transmission of information from a source or initiator without the source being requested to send that information. An example of a push technology is an SNMP trap. cf. pull technology.

PVC

CONTEXT [Fibre Channel]

Acronym for Permanent Virtual Circuit.

QoS

Acronym for quality of service.

quiesce (verb)

CONTEXT [Data Recovery]

To bring a device or an application to a state in which (a.) it is able to operate, (b.) all of its data is consistent and stored on non-volatile storage, and (c.) processing has been suspended and there are no tasks in progress (i.e., all application tasks have either been completed or not started).

quiescent state

CONTEXT [Data Recovery]

An application or device state in which (a.) the application or device is able to operate, (b.) all of its data is consistent and stored on non-volatile storage, and (c.) processing has been suspended and there are no tasks in progress (i.e., all tasks have either been completed or not started).

quality of service

CONTEXT [Management]

A technique for managing computer system resources such as bandwidth by specifying user visible parameters such as message delivery time. Policy rules are used to describe the operation of network elements to make these guarantees. Relevant standards for QoS in the IETF are the RSVP (Resource Reservation Protocol) and COPS (Common Open Policy Service) protocols. RSVP allows for the reservation of bandwidth in advance, while COPS allows routers and switches to obtain policy rules from a server.

RADIUS

CONTEXT [Security]

Acronym for Remote Authentication Dial In User Service.

RAID

CONTEXT [Storage System]

1. An Acronym for Redundant Array of Independent Disks, a family of techniques for managing multiple disks to deliver desirable cost, data availability, and performance characteristics to host environments.
2. A Redundant Array of Independent Disks.
3. A phrase adopted from the 1988 SIGMOD paper A Case for Redundant Arrays of Inexpensive Disks.

RAID 0

RAID Level 0

CONTEXT [Storage System]

Synonym for data striping.

RAID 1

RAID Level 1

CONTEXT [Storage System]

Synonym for mirroring.

RAID 2

RAID Level 2

CONTEXT [Storage System]

A form of RAID in which a Hamming code computed on stripes of data on some of an array's disks is stored on the remaining disks and serves as check data.

RAID 3

RAID Level 3

CONTEXT [Storage System]

A form of parity RAID in which all disks are assumed to be rotationally synchronized, and in which the data stripe size is no larger than the exported block size.

RAID 4

RAID Level 4

CONTEXT [Storage System]

A form of parity RAID in which the disks operate independently, the data strip size is no smaller than the exported block size, and all parity check data is stored on one disk.

RAID 5

RAID Level 5

CONTEXT [Storage System]

A form of parity RAID in which the disks operate independently, the data strip size is no smaller than the exported block size, and parity check data is distributed across the array's disks.

RAID 6

RAID Level 6

CONTEXT [Storage System]

Any form of RAID that can continue to execute read and write requests to all of an array's virtual disks in the presence of two concurrent disk failures. Both dual check data computations (parity and Reed Solomon) and orthogonal dual parity check data have been proposed for RAID Level 6.

RAID array
CONTEXT [Storage System]

Acronym for Redundant Array of Independent Disks.

RAMdisk
CONTEXT [Storage Device]

A quantity of host system random access memory (RAM) managed by software and presented to applications as a high-performance disk. RAMdisks generally emulate disk I/O functional characteristics, but unless augmented by special hardware to make their contents non-volatile, they cannot tolerate loss of power without losing data. cf. solid state disk

random I/O

random I/O load

random reads

random writes
CONTEXT [Storage System]

Any I/O load whose consecutively issued read and/or write requests do not specify adjacently located data. The term random I/O is commonly used to denote any I/O load that is not sequential, whether or not the distribution of data locations is indeed random. Random I/O is characteristic of I/O request-intensive applications. cf. sequential I/O.

random number
CONTEXT [Security]

An unpredictable number used for cryptographic applications that is typically a generated sequence of zero and one bits. There are two basic classes: deterministic or pseudorandom often generated by an algorithm that produces a sequence of bits from an initial value called a seed; and nondeterministic generated by some unpredictable physical source that is outside human control.

R

random relative offset

CONTEXT [Fibre Channel]

> A transmission control algorithm in which the frames containing the subblocks that comprise a block of information may be transmitted in any order. This complicates reassembly and detection of lost frames by comparison with continuously increasing relative offset.

rank

CONTEXT [Storage System]

1. A set of physical disk positions in an enclosure, usually denoting the disks that are or can be members of a single array.
2. The set of corresponding target identifiers on all of a controller's device I/O buses. Like the preceding definition, the disks identified as a rank by this definition usually are or can be members of a single array
3. Synonym for a stripe in a redundancy group. Because of the diversity of meanings attached to this term by disk subsystem developers, SNIA publications make minimal use of it.

RAS

1. Acronym for Reliability, Availability, and Serviceability
2. Acronym for Remote Access Server (Windows NT dialup networking server).

raw partition

> A disk partition not managed by a volume manager. The term raw partition is frequently encountered when discussing database systems because some database system vendors recommend volumes or files for underlying database storage, while others recommend direct storage on raw partitions.

raw partition backup

CONTEXT [Data Recovery]

> A bit-by-bit copy of a partition image. A raw partition backup incorporates no information about the objects contained on the partition, and hence cannot be used for individual object restoration. cf. disk image backup

read/write head

CONTEXT [Storage Device]

The magnetic or optical recording device in a disk. Read/write heads are used both to write data by altering the recording media's state, and to read data by sensing the alterations. Disks typically have read/write heads, unlike tapes, in which reading and writing are often done using separate heads.

real time copy

CONTEXT [Storage System]

Synonym for mirroring.

rebuild

rebuilding

CONTEXT [Storage System]

The regeneration and writing onto one or more replacement disks of all of the user data and check data from a failed disk in a mirrored or RAID array. In most arrays, a rebuild can occur while applications are accessing data on the array's virtual disks.

receiver

CONTEXT [Fibre Channel]

1. An interconnect or network device that includes a detector and signal processing electronics.
2. The portion of a Link_Control_Facility dedicated to receiving an encoded bit stream, converting the stream into transmission characters, and decoding the characters using the rules specified by FC-PH.
3. A circuit that converts an optical or electrical media signal to a (possibly retimed) electrical serial logic signal.

receptacle

The stationary (female) half of the interface connector on a transmitter or receiver.

reconstruction

CONTEXT [Storage System]

Synonym for rebuilding.

recorded volume serial number
CONTEXT [Data Recovery]

Synonym for media ID. Abbreviated RVSN.

recovery
CONTEXT [Data Recovery]

The recreation of a past operational state of an entire application or computing environment. Recovery is required after an application or computing environment has been destroyed or otherwise rendered unusable. It may include restoration of application data, if that data had been destroyed as well. cf. restoration

Recovery Point Objective
CONTEXT [Data Recovery]

The maximum desired time period prior to a failure or disaster during which changes to data may be lost as a consequence of recovery. Data changes preceding the failure or disaster by at least this time period are preserved by recovery. Zero is a valid value and is equivalent to a "zero data loss" requirement. Acronym RPO.

Recovery Time Objective – RTO
CONTEXT [Data Recovery]

The maximum desired time period required to bring one or more applications and associated data back to a correct operational state.

red
CONTEXT [Security]

In the context of security analysis, a designation applied to information systems and associated areas, circuits, components, and equipment in which sensitive information is being processed.

red/black concept
CONTEXT [Security]

The separation of electrical and electronic circuits, components, equipment and systems that handle sensitive information (red) in electrical form, from those that handle on information that is not sensitive (black) in the same form.

reduced mode
CONTEXT [Storage System]

Synonym for degraded mode.

reduction
CONTEXT [Storage System]

The removal of a member disk from a RAID array, placing the array in degraded mode. Reduction most often occurs because of member disk failure, however, some RAID implementations allow reduction for system management purposes.

redundancy

The inclusion of extra components of a given type in a system (beyond those required by the system to carry out its function) for the purpose of enabling continued operation in the event of a component failure.

redundancy group
CONTEXT [Management] [Storage System]

1. A collection of extents organized by for the purpose of providing data protection. Within a redundancy group, a single type of data protection is employed. All of the usable storage capacity in a redundancy group is protected by check data stored within the group, and no usable storage external to a redundancy group is protected by check data within it

2. A class defined in the CIM schema (CIM_RedundancyGroup) consisting of a collection of objects in which redundancy is provided. Three subclasses of CIM_RedundancyGroup are defined (1.) CIM_SpareGroup for sparing and failover, (2.) CIM_ExtraCapacityGroup for load sharing or load balancing, and (3.) CIM_StorageRedundancyGroup to describe the redundancy algorithm in use.

redundancy group stripe
CONTEXT [Storage System]

A set of sequences of correspondingly numbered physical extent blocks in each of the physical extents comprising a redundancy group. The check data blocks in a redundancy group stripe protect the protected space in that stripe.

redundancy group stripe depth

CONTEXT [Storage System]

The number of consecutively numbered physical extent blocks in one physical extent of a redundancy group stripe. In the conventional striped data mapping model, redundancy group stripe depth is the same for all stripes in a redundancy group.

redundant (components)

Components of a system that have the capability to substitute for each other when necessary, as, for example when one of the components fails, so that the system can continue to perform its function. In storage subsystems, power distribution units, power supplies, cooling devices, and controllers are often configured to be redundant. The disks comprising a mirror set are redundant. A parity RAID array's member disks are redundant, since surviving disks can collectively replace the function of a failed disk.

redundant (configuration, system)

A system or configuration of a system in which failure tolerance is achieved by the presence of redundant instances of all components that are critical to the system's operation.

Redundant Array of Independent Disks

CONTEXT [Storage System]

A disk array in which part of the physical storage capacity is used to store redundant information about user data stored on the remainder of the storage capacity. The redundant information enables regeneration of user data in the event that one of the array's member disks or the access path to it fails.

Although it does not conform to this definition, disk striping is often referred to as RAID (RAID Level 0).

Reference data

CONTEXT [Information Lifecycle Management]

Synonym for fixed content.

Reference information

CONTEXT [Information Lifecycle Management]

Synonym for fixed content.

regeneration

CONTEXT [Storage System]

Recreation of user data from a failed disk in a RAID array using check data and user data from surviving members. Regeneration may also be used to recover data from an unrecoverable media error. Data in a parity RAID array is regenerated by computing the exclusive OR of the contents of corresponding blocks from the array's remaining disks. Data in a RAID Level 6 array is regenerated by choosing the more convenient of two parity algorithms and executing it.

registered state change notification

CONTEXT [Fibre Channel]

A Fibre Channel switch function that allows notification to registered nodes if a change occurs to other specified nodes.

rejoin mirror

CONTEXT [Storage System]

Bring a split mirror component back into the mirror. When the resilvering process completes, the mirror component becomes identical to all mirror components in the mirror.

rekeying

CONTEXT [Security]

The process of changing the key used for an ongoing communication session.

relative offset

CONTEXT [Fibre Channel]

A displacement, expressed in bytes, used to divide a quantity of data into blocks and subblocks for transmission in separate frames. Relative offsets are used to reassemble data at the receiver and verify that all data has arrived.

relative offset space

CONTEXT [Fibre Channel]

A numerical range defined by a sending upper level protocol for an information category. The range starts at zero, representing the upper level-defined-origin, and extends to a highest value. Relative offset values are required to lie within the appropriate relative offset space.

Remote Authentication Dial In User Service

CONTEXT [Security]

RADIUS is an authentication and accounting protocol used by many Internet Service Providers (ISPs). Information such as username and password is entered when a connection is made. This information is passed to a RADIUS server that verifies the information in order to authorizes access to the system. Radius is defined in RFC 2865.

removable media storage device

A storage device designed so that its storage media can be readily removed and inserted. Tapes, CDROMs, and optical disks are removable media devices.

repeater

CONTEXT [Fibre Channel]

A circuit that uses clock recovered from an incoming signal to generate an outbound signal.

repeating ordered set

CONTEXT [Fibre Channel]

An ordered set issued by FC-2 to FC-1 for repeated transmission until a subsequent transmission request is issued by FC-2.

replacement disk

CONTEXT [Storage System]

A disk available for use as or used to replace a failed member disk in a RAID array.

replacement unit

A component or collection of components in a system which are always replaced (swapped) as a unit when any part of the collection fails. Abbreviated RU. Replacement units may be field replaceable, or they may require that the system of which they are part be returned to a factory or repair depot for replacement. Field replaceable units may be customer replaceable, or their replacement may require trained service personnel. Typical replacement units in a disk subsystem include disks, controller logic boards, power supplies, cooling devices, and cables. Replacement units may be cold, warm, or hot swappable.

replay attack

CONTEXT [Security]

An attack in which a valid data transmission is maliciously or fraudulently repeated, either by the originator or by an adversary who intercepts the data and retransmits it.

replica

CONTEXT [Data Recovery]

1. A general term for a copy of a collection of data. cf. duplicate, point in time copy, snapshot.
2. An image of data usable by one or more applications without an intermediate restore process. cf. backup copy.

replicate

CONTEXT [Data Recovery]

1. (noun) A general term for a copy of a collection of data. cf. duplicate, point in time copy, snapshot
2. (verb) The action of making a replicate as defined above.

replication link

CONTEXT [Storage System]

A physical and logical connection that transports data and replication control commands between primary and secondary sites.

replication set

CONTEXT [Storage System]

A pair of volumes that have a replication relationship. A replication set consists of a primary volume and a secondary volume that are physically separated. The replication set also defines how the primary and secondary volumes are connected and how replication ought to proceed.

Request for Comment

CONTEXT [Security]

Internet -related specifications, including standards, experimental definitions, informational documents and best practice definitions, produced by the IETF.

request intensive (application)

A characterization of applications. A request-intensive application is an I/O intensive application characterized by a high rate of I/O requests. Request-intensive applications' I/O requests are usually randomly addressed and often specify a small amount of data for transfer.

reserved (field)

CONTEXT [Fibre Channel]

1. In a standard, a field in a data structure set aside for future definition. Some standards prescribe implementation behavior with respect to reserved fields (e.g., originators of data structures containing reserved fields must zero fill them; consumers of data structures containing reserved fields must ignore them, etc.); others do not.

2. A field filled with binary zeros by a source N_Port and ignored by a destination N_Port. Each bit in a reserved field is denoted by "r" in the Fibre Channel standards. Future enhancements to FC-PH may define usages for reserved fields. Implementations should not check or interpret reserved fields. Violation of this guideline may result in loss of compatibility with future implementations which comply with future enhancements to FC-PH.

resilvering

CONTEXT [Backup] [Storage Systems]

Synonym for mirror resynchronization.

responder

CONTEXT [General] [Fibre Channel]

1. [General] In a negotiation or exchange, the party that responds to the originator of the negotiation or exchange.

2. [Fibre Channel] Synonym for target. Used only in Fibre Channel contexts.

Responder Exchange Identifier

CONTEXT [Fibre Channel]

An identifier assigned by a responder to identify an exchange. Abbreviated RX_ID. An RX_ID is meaningful only to the responder that originates it.

restoration

CONTEXT [Data Recovery]

The copying of a backup to on-line storage for application use.
Restoration normally occurs after part or all of an application's data has
been destroyed or become inaccessible. cf. recovery

retention period

CONTEXT [Data Recovery] [File System]

1. [Data Recovery] The length of time that a backup image should be kept.
2. [File System] In some file systems, such as that shipped with IBM
    Corporation's OS/390 operating system, a property of a file that can
    be used to implement backup and data migration policies.

Retention policy

CONTEXT [Information Lifecycle Management]

A policy governing when and for how long a record must be retained by a
storage system. This may be a rule that applies to groups or categories of
records, or may be specified for individual records. The policy may be
time or event based.

retimer

CONTEXT [Fibre Channel]

A circuit that uses a clock independent of the incoming signal to generate
an outbound signal.

return loss

CONTEXT [Fibre Channel]

The ratio of the strength of a returned signal to that of the incident signal
that caused it. In electrical circuits, return loss is caused by impedance
discontinuities. Optical return loss is caused by index of refraction differ-
ences.

reverse rejoin mirror

CONTEXT [Storage System]

Operation performed on a split mirror component, in order to use its data
as the basis for the mirror as a whole. When a component is reverse
rejoined, all mirror components in the mirror become identical to the
previously split mirror component as a result of the resilver process.

RFC
CONTEXT [Security]

> Acronym for Request for Comment.

risk
CONTEXT [Security]

> The potential that a given threat will exploit vulnerabilities of an asset or group of assets to cause loss or damage to the assets [IEEE 13335-1:1996].

risk analysis
CONTEXT [Security]

> The process of identifying security risks, determining their magnitude, and identifying areas needing safeguards [IEEE 13335-1:1996].

risk management
CONTEXT [Security]

> The process of assessing and quantifying risk and establishing an acceptable level of risk for the organization [IEEE 13335-1:1996].

robot

robotic media handler
CONTEXT [Data Recovery]

> A mechanical handler capable of storing multiple pieces of removable media and loading and unloading them from one or more drives in arbitrary order in response to electronic commands. cf. library.

rollback to snapshot
CONTEXT [Storage System]

> The process of resetting a volume's data to become identical to a snapshot taken of that volume.

rotational latency

CONTEXT [Storage Device]

> The interval between the end of a disk seek and the time at which the starting block address specified in the I/O request passes the disk head. Exact rotational latencies for specific sequences of I/O operations can only be obtained by detailed disk drive simulation or measurement. The simplifying assumption that on average, requests wait for half a disk revolution time of rotational latency works well in practice. Half of a disk revolution time is therefore defined to be the average rotational latency.

row

CONTEXT [Storage System]

> The set of blocks with corresponding physical extent block addresses in each of an array's member physical extents. The concept of rows is useful for locking the minimal amount of data during a RAID array update so as to maximize the potential for parallel execution.

RPO

CONTEXT [Data Recovery]

> Acronym for Recovery Point Objective.

RSA

CONTEXT [Security]

> Acronym for both a public key algorithm and a corporation in the business of algorithm design, derived from the names of the founders (Rivest, Shamir & Adelman).

RSCN

CONTEXT [Fibre Channel]

> Acronym for registered state change notification.

RTO

CONTEXT [Data Recovery]

> Acronym for Recovery Time Objective.

RU

> Acronym for replaceable unit. cf. CRU, FRU

run length

The number of consecutive identical bits in a transmitted signal. For
example, the pattern 0011111010 has run lengths of 2, 5, 1, 1, and 1.

running disparity

CONTEXT [Fibre Channel]

The cumulative disparity (positive or negative) of all previously issued
transmission characters.

RVSN

CONTEXT [Data Recovery]

Acronym for recorded volume serial number.

S_ID

CONTEXT [Fibre Channel]

Acronym for Source Identifier.

S_Port

CONTEXT [Fibre Channel]

A logical port inside a switch addressable by external N_Ports for service
functions. An S_Port may be an implicit switch port or a separate entity
such as a name server connected to and controlled by the switch.
S_Ports have well known port names to facilitate early discovery by
N_Ports.

SA

CONTEXT [Security]

Acronym for Security Association.

SAM

CONTEXT [SCSI]

Acronym for SCSI Architecture Model.

SAN

CONTEXT [Fibre Channel] [iSCSI][Network] [Storage System]

1. Acronym for storage area network. (This is the normal usage in SNIA documents.)
2. Acronym for Server Area Network which connects one or more servers.
3. Acronym for System Area Network for an interconnected set of system elements.

SAN attached storage

A term used to refer to storage elements that connect directly to a storage area network and provide file, database, block, or other types of data access services to computer systems. Abbreviated SAS. SAS elements that provide file access services are commonly called Network Attached Storage, or NAS devices. cf. NAS.

SAR

CONTEXT [Security]

Acronym for Security Assurance Requirements.

SAS

Acronym for SAN attached storage.

SATA

Acronym for Serial Advanced Technology Attachment.

saturated disk

A disk whose instantaneous I/O load is as great as or greater than its capability to satisfy the requests comprising the load. Mathematically, a saturated disk's I/O queue eventually becomes indefinitely long. In practice, however, user reaction or other system factors generally reduce the rate of new request arrival for a saturated disk.

scale (verb)

In computer systems, to grow or support growth in such a way that all capabilities of the system remain in constant ratio to each other. For example, a storage subsystem whose data transfer capacity increases by the addition of buses as its storage capacity increases by the addition of disks is said to scale.

schema

A collection of information models or data models.

script

1. A parameterized list of primitive I/O bus operations intended to be executed in sequence. Often used with respect to ports, most of which are able to execute scripts of I/O commands autonomously (without policy processor assistance).
2. A sequence of instructions intended to be parsed and carried out by another program. Perl, VBScript, JavaScript and Tcl are all scripting languages.

SCSI

CONTEXT [SCSI]

Acronym for Small Computer System Interface.

SCSI adapter

CONTEXT [SCSI]

An adapter that connects an intelligent device to a SCSI bus. cf. HBA, host bus adapter

SCSI address

CONTEXT [SCSI]

The full address used by a computer to communicate with a SCSI device, including an adapter number (required with computers configured with multiple SCSI adapters), and the target ID of the device. SCSI addresses do not include logical unit number, because those are not used for communication.

SCSI Architecture Model

CONTEXT [SCSI]

An ANSI standard that defines the generic requirements and overall framework in which other SCSI standards are defined. New generations of this standard are identified by a numeric suffix; for example the second generation standard is SAM2.

SCSI bus
CONTEXT [SCSI]

> Any parallel (multi-signal) I/O bus that implements some version of the ANSI SCSI standard. A wide SCSI bus may connect up to16 initiators and targets. A narrow SCSI bus may connect up to eight initiators and targets. cf. initiator, target.

SCSI Device
CONTEXT [SCSI]

> This is the SAM-2 term for an entity that contains other SCSI entities. For example, a SCSI Initiator Device contains one or more SCSI Initiator Ports and zero or more application clients.

SCSI Enclosure Services
CONTEXT [SCSI]

> An ANSI X3T10 standard for management of environmental factors such as temperature, power, voltage, etc. Abbreviated SES.

SCSI Initiator Port
CONTEXT [SCSI]

> The initiator endpoint of an I_T nexus.

SCSI Parallel Interface
CONTEXT [SCSI]

> The family of SCSI standards that define the characteristics of the parallel version of the SCSI interface. Abbreviated SPI. Several versions of SPI, known as SPI, SPI2, SPI3, etc., have been developed. Each version provides for greater performance and functionality than preceding ones.

SCSI Port
CONTEXT [SCSI]

> This is the SAM-2 term for an entity in a SCSI Device that provides the SCSI functionality to interface with a service delivery subsystem or transport.

SCSI Target Port
CONTEXT [SCSI]

> The target endpoint of an I_T nexus.

SCSI Trade Association

A trade association incorporated 1996 to promote all forms of SCSI technology in the market. Abbreviated STA. cf. http://www.scsita.org/

SDH

CONTEXT [Network]

Acronym for Synchronous Digital Hierarchy.

sector

CONTEXT [Storage Device]

S

The unit in which data is physically stored and protected against errors on a fixed block architecture disk. A sector typically consists of a synchronization pattern, a header field containing the block's address, data, a checksum or error correcting code, and a trailer. Adjacent sectors are often separated by information used to assist in track centering. Most often, each sector holds a block of data. cf. disk block

secure hash

CONTEXT [Security]

An algorithm that generates a digest from its input (e.g., a message). The digest has the properties that different inputs are extraordinarily unlikely to have the same fingerprint, small changes in its input lead to large changes in its output, and it is computationally intractable to generate an input that has the same fingerprint as a given input.

Secure Hash Algorithm 1

CONTEXT [Security]

A message digest algorithm that produces a 160 bit digest. SHA-1 is defined in RFC3174. Acronym SHA-1.

Secure Remote Password

CONTEXT [Security]

An authentication and key exchange system. Standardized by the Internet Engineering Task Force and described in RFC 2945. Acronym SRP.

Secure Sockets Layer

CONTEXT [Security]

> A suite of cyrptographic algorithms, protocols and procedures used to provide security for communications used to access the world wide web. The characters "https:" at the front of a URL cause SSL to be used to enhance communications security. More recent versions of SSL are known as TLS (Transport Level Security) and are standardized by the Internet Engineering Task Force (IETF).

security association

CONTEXT [Security]

> A simplex "connection" that affords security services to the traffic carried by it. To secure typical, bi-directional communication between two hosts, or between two security gateways, two Security Associations (one in each direction) are required. In IPsec, a security association is uniquely identified by a triple consisting of a Security Parameters Index (SPI), an IP Destination Address, and a security protocol identifier (Authentication Header or Encapsulating Security Payload). Acronym SA.

Security Assurance Requirements

CONTEXT [Security]

> A set of assurance components (classes and families) that represent a standard way of expressing the assurance requirements for TOEs. These requirements are drawn from ISO 15408-3:1999, whenever possible. Acronym SAR.

Security Functional Requirements

CONTEXT [Security]

> A set of security functional components (classes and families) that represent a standard way of expressing the functional requirements for TOEs. These requirements are drawn from ISO 15408-2:1999, whenever possible. Acronym SFR.

Security Parameters Index

CONTEXT [Security]

> A 32-bit number used to uniquely identify a security association (SA). In IP Security, SPI values must be synchronized between endpoints for the security functions to work properly. SPI values 1 through 255 have been reserved for use with standard implementations. Acronym SPI.

security safeguards

CONTEXT [Security]

> The protective measures and controls that are prescribed to meet the
> security requirements specified for a system. Those safeguards may
> include but are not necessarily limited to: hardware and software security
> features, operating procedures, accountability procedures, access and
> distribution controls, management constraints, personnel security, and
> physical structures, areas, and devices. Also called safeguards.

Security Target

CONTEXT [Security]

> A set of security functional and assurance requirements and specifica-
> tions to be used as the basis for evaluation of an identified product or
> system. It is most commonly associated with ISO 15408. Acronym ST.

SEQ_ID

Sequence Identifier

CONTEXT [Fibre Channel]

> A number transmitted with each data frame in a sequence that identifies
> the frame as part of the sequence.

sequence

CONTEXT [Fibre Channel]

> A set of Fibre Channel data frames with a common Sequence_ID
> (SEQ_ID), corresponding to one message element, block, or Information
> Unit. Sequences are transmitted from initiator to recipient, with an
> acknowledgment, if applicable, transmitted from recipient to initiator. cf.
> Sequence Initiator, Sequence Recipient

sequence initiative

CONTEXT [Fibre Channel]

> A Fibre Channel protocol feature that designates which end of an
> exchange has authority to send the next sequence.

Sequence Initiator

CONTEXT [Fibre Channel]

> An N_Port which initiates a sequence and transmits data frames to a des-
> tination N_Port. cf. Sequence Recipient

Sequence Recipient

CONTEXT [Fibre Channel]

> An N_Port or NL_Port which receives Data frames from a Sequence Initiator and, if applicable, transmits responses (Link Control frames) to the Sequence Initiator.

Sequence Status Block

CONTEXT [Fibre Channel]

> A data structure which tracks the state of a sequence. Both Sequence Initiators and Sequence Recipients have Sequence Status Blocks for each active sequence.

sequential I/O

sequential I/O load

sequential reads

sequential writes

> An I/O load consisting of consecutively issued read or write requests to adjacently located data. Sequential I/O is characteristic of data transfer intensive applications. cf. random I/O

SERDES

> Acronym for Serializer Deserializer.

serial (transmission)

CONTEXT [Fibre Channel]

> The transmission of data bits one at a time over a single link.

serial adapter

> An adapter that connects an intelligent device to an RS232 or RS425 serial communications link. Serial adapters are sometimes used by storage sub-systems, filers, and other intelligent devices to connect to serial consoles for management purposes. cf. adapter, host adapter.

Serial Advanced Technology Attachment

Serial ATA (SATA) is the evolution of the ATA interface from a parallel bus to serial connection architecture. Acronym SATA.

serial console

A real or emulated communication terminal used by humans to manage an intelligent device. Serial consoles connect to the devices' serial adapters.

serial SCSI

CONTEXT [SCSI]

Any implementation of SCSI that uses serial data transmission (as opposed to multi-conductor parallel buses). Optical and electrical Fibre Channel, SSA and IEEE 1394 are examples of serial SCSI implementations.

serializer deserializer

A mechanism for converting data from parallel to serial form and from serial to parallel form.

server

1. An intelligent device, usually a computer, that provides services to other intelligent devices, usually other computers or appliances. cf. client

2. An asymmetric relationship with a second party (a client) in which the client initiates requests and the server responds to those requests.

server based virtualization

Virtualization implemented in a host computer rather than in a storage subsystem or storage appliance. Virtualization can be implemented either in host computers, in storage subsystems or storage appliances, or in a specific virtualization appliances in the storage interconnect fabric.

serverless backup

CONTEXT [Data Recovery]

A backup methodology that utilizes a device other than the server to copy data without using the LAN. The copy may be performed by a network-attached controller (e.g., utilizing SCSI Extended Copy), by an appliance within the SAN, or by a Backup Server.

Server Message Block (protocol)

CONTEXT [Network]

A network file system access protocol designed primarily used by Windows clients to communicate file access requests to Windows servers. Abbreviated SMB. Current versions of the SMB protocol are usually referred to as CIFS, the Common Internet File System.

Service Incident Standard

CONTEXT [Management]

A DMTF standard that defines how a support or help desk incident is processed.

Service Level Agreement

An agreement between a service provider, such as an IT department, an internet services provider, or an intelligent device acting as a server, and a service consumer. A service level agreement defines parameters for measuring the service, and states quantitative values for those parameters. Abbreviated SLA.

Service Level Objective

Partitions an SLA into individual metrics and operational information to enforce and/or monitor the SLA. "Service Level Objectives" may be defined as part of an SLA, an SLS, or in a separate document. It is a set of parameters and their values. The actions of enforcing and reporting monitored compliance can be implemented as one or more policies. (See also "Service Level Agreement".)

Service Location Protocol

An IETF standards track protocol that provides a framework to allow networking applications to dynamically discover the existence, location, and configuration of networked services in enterprise networks. Acronym SLP.

SES

CONTEXT [SCSI] [Standards]

1. Acronym for SCSI Enclosure Services
2. Acronym for Solution Exchange Standard.

SFR

CONTEXT [Security]

Acronym for Security Functional Requirements.

SHA-1
CONTEXT [Security]

Acronym for Secure Hash Algorithm 1.

share
CONTEXT [File System]

A resource such as data or a printer device made available for use by users on other computer systems. For example, a printer or a collection of files stored in a single directory tree on a file server may be made available as a share. CIFS clients, which include most networked personal computers, typically map a share to a drive letter.

shielded enclosure
CONTEXT [Security]

A room or container designed to attenuate electromagnetic radiation.

shelf
CONTEXT [Storage System]

A modular enclosure for storage devices (disks and tapes). Storage shelves usually contain power supplies and cooling devices, and have pre-wired backplanes that carry power and I/O bus signals to the devices mounted in them. cf. canister

SIA
1. Acronym for Semiconductor Industries Association.
2. Acronym for SCSI Industry Association.

simple name server
CONTEXT [Fibre Channel] [Network]

A service provided by a Fibre Channel switch that simplifies discovery of devices attached to the fabric.

Simple Network Management Protocol
CONTEXT [Network] [Standards]

An IETF protocol for monitoring and managing systems and devices in a network. The data being monitored and managed is defined by a MIB. The functions supported by the protocol are the request and retrieval of data, the setting or writing of data, and traps that signal the occurrence of events.

single (component) configuration

A configuration in which the referenced component is not redundant. cf. redundant (component)

single ended (signaling)

CONTEXT [SCSI]

An electrical signaling technique in which all control and data signals are represented by a voltage difference from a common ground. cf. differential

single mode (fiber optic cable)

CONTEXT [Fibre Channel] [Network]

A fiber optic cabling specification that provides for up to 10 kilometer distance between devices.

single point of failure

One component or path in a system, the failure of which would make the system inoperable. Acronym SPOF.

SIS

CONTEXT [Management] [Standards]

Acronym for Service Incident Standard.

SLA

Acronym for Service Level Agreement.

SLO

Acronym for Service Level Objective.

SLP

Acronym for Service Location Protocol.

Small Computer System Interface (SCSI)

CONTEXT [SCSI]

A collection of ANSI standards and proposed standards which define I/O buses primarily intended for connecting storage subsystems or devices to hosts through host bus adapters. Originally intended primarily for use with small (desktop and desk-side workstation) computers, SCSI has been extended to serve most computing needs, and is arguably the most widely implemented I/O bus in use today.

small read request

small write request

small I/O request

An I/O, read, or write request that specifies the transfer of a relatively small amount of data. 'Small' usually depends on the context, but most often refers to 8 KBytes or fewer. cf. large I/O request

SMB

CONTEXT [File System] [Network]

Acronym for Server Message Block.

SMI

CONTEXT [SNIA] [Fibre Channel] [Management] [Network]

1. [SNIA] The Storage Networking Industry Association's (SNIA) Storage Management Initiative (SMI) develops and standardizes interoperable storage management technologies, including providing conformance testing for products.
2. [Fibre Channel] [Management] [Network] Acronym for Structure of Management Information.

SMI-S

CONTEXT [SNIA][Standards]

Acronym for Storage Management Initiative – Specification.

SMPTE

CONTEXT [Standards]

Acronym for Society of Motion Picture and Television Engineers.

snapshot

CONTEXT [Data Recovery] [Storage System]

A fully usable copy of a defined collection of data that contains an image of the data as it appeared at the point in time at which the copy was initiated. A snapshot may be either a duplicate or a replicate of the data it represents.

SNIA

CONTEXT [Network] [Standards] [Storage System]

Acronym for Storage Networking Industry Association.

sniffer
CONTEXT [Security]

>A software tool for auditing and identifying network traffic packets.

SNMP
CONTEXT [Network] [Management]

>Acronym for Simple Network Management Protocol.

SNS
CONTEXT [Network]

>Acronym for Simple Name Server.

Society of Motion Picture and Television Engineers
CONTEXT [Standards]

>An industry association whose goal is to standardize television and motion picture industry information interchange protocols.

soft zone
CONTEXT [Fibre Channel]

>A zone consisting of zone members that are permitted to communicate with each other via the fabric.

>Soft zones are typically implemented through a combination of name server and Fibre Channel protocol -- when a port contacts the name server, the name server returns information only about Fibre Channel ports in the same zone(s) as the requesting port. This prevents ports outside the zone(s) from being discovered and hence the Fibre Channel protocol will not attempt to communicate with such ports. In contrast to hard zones, soft zones are not enforced by hardware; e.g., a frame that is erroneously addressed to a port that should not receive it will nonetheless be delivered. Well known addresses {link} are implicitly included in every zone. cf. zone, hard zone

SOF
CONTEXT [Fibre Channel]

>Acronym for start of frame.

solicited control
CONTEXT [Fibre Channel]

>An information category indicated in a Fibre Channel frame header.

solicited data

CONTEXT [Fibre Channel]

An information category indicated in a Fibre Channel frame header.

solid state disk

CONTEXT [Storage Device]

A disk whose storage capability is provided by solid-state random access memory rather than magnetic or optical media. A solid state disk generally offers very high access performance compared to that of rotating magnetic disks, because it eliminates mechanical seek and rotation time. It may also offer very high data transfer capacity. Cost per byte of storage, however, is typically quite high, and volumetric density is lower. A solid state disk include some mechanism such as battery backup or magnetic backing store that allows its operating environment to treat it as non-volatile storage. cf. RAMdisk

Solution Exchange Standard

CONTEXT [Management]

A DMTF standard that defines the exchange of support or help desk information.

SONET

CONTEXT [Network]

Acronym for Synchronous Optical Network.

Source Identifier

CONTEXT [Fibre Channel]

A number in a Fibre Channel frame that identifies the source of the frame. Abbreviated S_ID. cf. D_ID

source N_Port

CONTEXT [Fibre Channel]

The N_Port from which a frame is transmitted.

spare (disk, extent)

CONTEXT [Storage System]

An object reserved for the purpose of substitution for a like object in case of that object's failure.

special character

CONTEXT [Fibre Channel]

> Any transmission character that is valid in the transmission code but does not correspond to a valid data byte. Special characters are used to denote special functions.

special code

CONTEXT [Fibre Channel]

> A code which, when encoded using the rules specified by the transmission code, results in a special character. Special codes are typically associated with control signals related to protocol management (e.g., K28.5).

SPI

CONTEXT [SCSI] [Security]

1. [SCSI] Acronym for SCSI Parallel Interface.
2. [Security] Acronym for Security Parameters Index.

spiral data transfer rate

> Synonym for full volume transfer rate.

split I/O request

1. An I/O request to a virtual disk which requires two or more I/O operations to satisfy, because the virtual data addresses in the request map to more than one extent on one or more disks
2. An application I/O request that is divided into two or more sub-requests by a file system or other operating system component because the amount of data requested is too large for the operating environment to handle as a unit.

split mirror

split mirror copy

split mirror point in time copy
CONTEXT [Storage System]

> Any of a class of point in time copy implementations or the resulting
> copies in which the storage for the copy is synchronized to the source of
> the copy and then split. A split mirror copy occupies as much storage as
> the source of the copy.

CONTEXT [Data Recovery]

> A method for generating a frozen image of a set of data. A split mirror
> frozen image is a set of storage devices containing a complete copy of
> data as of the moment of frozen image creation. When a split mirror
> frozen image has served its purpose, the contents of the storage devices
> it occupies must be resynchronized with the original data from which it
> was split.

SPOF

> Acronym for Single Point Of Failure.

spoofing
CONTEXT [Security]

> Unauthorized use of legitimate identification and authentication data to
> mimic a subject different from the attacker. Impersonating, masquerading,
> piggybacking and mimicking are forms of spoofing.

SR
CONTEXT [Fibre Channel]

> Acronym for Sequence Recipient.

SRM
CONTEXT [Management]

> Acronym for storage resource management.

SRP
CONTEXT [Security]

> Acronym for Secure Remote Password.

SSID
CONTEXT [iSCSI]

> Acronym for iSCSI Session Identifier.

ST
CONTEXT [Security]

> Acronym for Security Target.

STA

> Acronym for SCSI Trade Association.

stand alone drive
CONTEXT [Data Recovery]

> A removable media drive that is not associated with a media stacker or robot.

standard interconnect
CONTEXT [Standards]

> An I/O or network interconnect whose specifications are readily available to the public, and which can therefore easily be implemented in a vendor's products without license or royalty payments. Also called open interconnect.

star

> A physical network configuration in which every node is connected directly to, and only to, a central point. All communications pass through the central point, which may be a hub or a switch.

start of frame
CONTEXT [Fibre Channel]

> A group of ordered sets that delineates the beginning of a frame.

storage area network

CONTEXT [Fibre Channel] [Network] [Storage System]

1. A network whose primary purpose is the transfer of data between computer systems and storage elements and among storage elements. Abbreviated SAN. A SAN consists of a communication infrastructure, which provides physical connections, and a management layer, which organizes the connections, storage elements, and computer systems so that data transfer is secure and robust. The term SAN is usually (but not necessarily) identified with block I/O services rather than file access services.

2. A storage system consisting of storage elements, storage devices, computer systems, and/or appliances, plus all control software, communicating over a network.

NOTE: The SNIA definition specifically does not identify the term SAN with Fibre Channel technology. When the term SAN is used in connection with Fibre Channel technology, use of a qualified phrase such as "Fibre Channel SAN" is encouraged. According to this definition an Ethernet-based network whose primary purpose is to provide access to storage elements would be considered a SAN. SANs are sometimes also used for system interconnection in clusters.

storage array

CONTEXT [Storage System]

A collection of disks or tapes from one or more commonly accessible storage subsystems, combined with a body of control software.

storage controller

CONTEXT [Storage System]

An intelligent controller to which storage devices are attached.

storage device

CONTEXT [Storage Device]

A collective term for disks, tapes, disk arrays, tape arrays, and any other mechanisms capable of non-volatile data storage. This definition is specifically intended to exclude aggregating storage elements such as RAID array subsystems, robotic tape libraries, filers, and file servers.

storage device virtualization

Virtualization of storage devices such as disk, tape drive, RAID shelves, etc.

storage domain
CONTEXT [Storage System]

> A collection of storage resources and supporting software and interfaces that are managed as a unit.

storage element

> Any device designed and built primarily for the purpose of persistent data storage and delivery. This definition is specifically intended to encompass disk drives, tape drives, RAID array subsystems, robotic tape libraries, filers, file servers, and any other types of storage devices.

storage extent

> A CIM object called CIM_StorageExtent. A storage extent instance may represent either removable or nonremoveable media. cf. extent.

Storage Management Initiative – Specification
CONTEXT [SNIA][Standards]

> A standard storage management interface developed by SNIA. Acronym SMI-S.

storage networking

> The practice of creating, installing, administering, or using networks whose primary purpose is the transfer of data between computer systems and storage elements and among storage elements.

Storage Networking Industry Association
CONTEXT [Network] [Standards] [Storage System]

> An association of producers and consumers of storage networking products whose goal is to further storage networking technology and applications Acronym SNIA.

storage resource management
CONTEXT [Management]

> Management of physical and logical storage resources, including storage elements, storage devices, appliances, virtual devices, disk volume and file resources.

storage security
CONTEXT [Security]

> Technical controls that protect storage resources and data from unauthorized users and may include integrity, confidentiality and availability of the those resources and data.

storage subsystem
CONTEXT [Storage System]

> An integrated collection of (a.) storage controllers and/or host bus adapters, (b.) storage devices such as disks, CDROMs, tapes, media loaders and robots, and (c.) any required control software, that provides storage services to one or more computers.

storage subsystem virtualization

> The implementation of virtualization in a storage subsystem.
> storage virtualization
> 1. The act of abstracting, hiding, or isolating the internal function of a storage (sub) system or service from applications, compute servers or general network resources for the purpose of enabling application and network independent management of storage or data.
> 2. The application of virtualization to storage services or devices for the purpose of aggregating, hiding complexity or adding new capabilities to lower level storage resources.
>
> Storage can be virtualized simultaneously in multiple layers of a system, for instance to create HSM like systems.

storage volume

> In CIM, a StorageVolume is a subclass of CIM_StorageExtent and represents an object presented to an operating system, for example, by a hardware RAID cabinet), to a file system (for example, by a software volume manager) or to another entity. Storage volumes do NOT participate in CIM_StorageRedundancyGroups. They are directly realized in hardware or are the end result of assembling and building on lower level extents.

store and forward (switching)
CONTEXT [Fibre Channel] [Network]

> A switching technique that requires buffering an entire frame before a routing decision is made.

streamed sequence

CONTEXT [Fibre Channel]

A new sequence initiated by a Sequence Initiator in any class of service for an exchange while it already has sequences open for that exchange.

strip

CONTEXT [Storage System]

A number of consecutively addressed blocks in a single extent. A disk array's uses strips to map virtual disk block addresses to member disk block addresses. Also known as stripe element.

strip size

CONTEXT [Storage System]

Synonym for stripe depth.

stripe

CONTEXT [Storage System]

The set of strips at corresponding locations of each member extent of a disk array which uses striped data mapping. The strips in a stripe are associated with each other in a way (e.g., relative extent block addresses) that allows membership in the stripe to be quickly and uniquely determined by a computational algorithm. Parity RAID uses uses stripes to map virtual disk block addresses to member extent block addresses.

stripe depth

CONTEXT [Storage System]

The number of blocks in a strip in a disk array which uses striped data mapping. Also, the number of consecutively addressed virtual disk blocks mapped to consecutively addressed blocks on a single member extent of a disk array.

stripe element

CONTEXT [Storage System]

Synonym for strip.

stripe size
CONTEXT [Storage System]

> The number of blocks in a stripe. A striped array's stripe size is the stripe depth multiplied by the number of member extents. A parity RAID array's stripe size is the stripe depth multiplied by one less than the number of member extents.

striped array

striped disk array
CONTEXT [Storage System]

> A disk array with striped data mapping but no redundancy for failure protection. Striped arrays are usually used to improve I/O performance on data that is of low value or easily replaced.

stripeset
CONTEXT [Storage System]

> Synonym for striped array.

striping
CONTEXT [Storage System]

> 1. Short for data striping; also known as RAID Level 0 or RAID 0. A mapping technique in which fixed-size consecutive ranges of virtual disk data addresses are mapped to successive array members in a cyclic pattern
> 2. A network technique for aggregating the bandwidth of several links between the same pair of nodes. A single data stream can be spread across the links for higher aggregate bandwidth. Sometimes called port aggregation.

Structure of Management Information
CONTEXT [Fibre Channel] [Management] [Network]

> A notation for setting or retrieving management variables over SNMP.

SSL
CONTEXT [Security]

> Acronym for Secure Sockets Layer

subdirectory
CONTEXT [File System]

> A directory in a hierarchical directory tree whose parent is a directory.

subject
CONTEXT [Security]

> In the context of access control or authorization, an entity whose access or usage is controlled. Users are examples of subjects.

substitution

> The assumption of a component's function in a system by a functionally equivalent component.

SVC
CONTEXT [Network]

> Acronym for Switched Virtual Circuit.

swap

swapping

> The installation of a replacement unit in place of a defective unit in a system. Units are any parts of a system which may either field replaceable (FRUs) by a vendor service representative or consumer replaceable (CRUs).
>
> A physical swap operation may be cold, warm, or hot, depending on the state in which the disk subsystem must be in order to perform it. A functional swap operation may be an auto swap or it may require human intervention.

switch
CONTEXT [Fibre Channel] [Network]

> A network infrastructure component to which multiple nodes attach. Unlike hubs, switches typically have internal bandwidth that is a multiple of link bandwidth, and the ability to rapidly switch node connections from one to another. A typical switch can accommodate several simultaneous full link bandwidth transmissions between different pairs of nodes. cf. hub

switch-back

Synonym for failback.

switch-over

Synonym for failover.

switched over (system)

Synonym for failed over.

symmetric cryptosystem

CONTEXT [Security]

A cryptographic algorithm in which the same key is used to encrypt and decrypt a single message or block of stored information. Keys used in a symmetric cryptosystem must be kept secret.

symmetric virtualization

Synonym for in-band virtualization. In-band virtualization is the preferred term

Synchronous Digital Hierarchy

CONTEXT [Network]

An ISO standard with 155, 622, 2048, 9953 Mbps serial data rates in steps of 4. A common worldwide telecommunications methodology. SDH uses a light scrambling of data to remove only the lowest frequency elements with the goal of achieving maximum digital bandwidth use.

synchronization

CONTEXT [Fibre Channel]

1. A receiver's identification of a transmission word boundary
2. The act of aligning or making two entities be equivalent at a specified point in time.

synchronize

CONTEXT [Storage System]

In the context of data replication, to establish an identical copy of the user data on the primary volume onto the secondary volume.

synchronous operations

Operations which have a fixed time relationship to each other. Most commonly used to denote I/O operations which occur in time sequence, i.e., a successor operation does not occur until its predecessor is complete.

Synchronous Optical Network

CONTEXT [Network]

> A standard for optical network elements. Abbreviated SONET. SONET provides modular building blocks, fixed overheads, integrated operations channels, and flexible payload mappings. Basic SONET provides a bandwidth of 51.840 megabits/second. This is known as OC-1. Higher bandwidths that are n times the basic rate are available (known as OC-n). OC-3, OC-12, OC-48, and OC-192 are currently in common use.

synchronous replication

CONTEXT [Storage System]

> A replication technique in which data must be committed to stable storage at both the primary site and the secondary site before the write is acknowledged to the host.system board.
>
> A printed circuit module containing mounting devices for processor(s), memory, and adapter cards, and implementing basic computer functions such as memory access, processor and I/O bus clocking, and human interface device attachment.

system disk

> The disk on which a computer system's operating software is stored. The system disk is usually the disk from which the operating system is boot-strapped (initially loaded into memory). The system disk frequently contains the computer system's swap and/or page files as well. It may also contain libraries of common software shared among several applications

system under test

> An entity being tested to verify functional behavior or determine performance characteristics. Distinguished from test system.

T1 copy
CONTEXT [Storage System]

Synonym for mirroring.

T10
CONTEXT [SCSI]

The ANSI T10 technical committee, the standards organization responsible for SCSI standards for communication between computers and storage subsystems and devices.

T11
CONTEXT [Fibre Channel]

The ANSI T11 technical committee, the standards organization responsible for Fibre Channel and certain other standards for moving electronic data into and out of computers and intelligent storage subsystems and devices.

tabular mapping
CONTEXT [Storage System]

A form of mapping in which a lookup table contains the correspondence between the two address spaces being mapped to each other. If a mapping between two address spaces is tabular, there is no mathematical formula that will convert addresses in one space to addresses in the other. cf. algorithmic mapping, dynamic mapping.

tampering
CONTEXT [Security]

>An unauthorized modification that alters the proper functioning of a device, system or communications path in a manner that degrades the security or functionality it provides.

tape

tape drive

tape transport
CONTEXT [Storage Device]

>A storage device that writes data sequentially in the order in which it is delivered, and reads data in the order in which it is stored on the media. Unlike disks, tapes use implicit data addressing. cf. disk

tape array
CONTEXT [Storage System]

>A collection of tapes from one or more commonly accessible storage sub-systems, combined with a body of control software.

tape virtualization

tape drive virtualization

tape library virtualization

>The act of creating abstracted tape devices by applying virtualization to tape drives or tape libraries.

target
CONTEXT [SCSI]

>The system component that receives a SCSI I/O command command. cf. initiator, LUN, target ID

target ID
CONTEXT [SCSI]

>The SCSI bus address of a target device or controller.

Target of Evaluation
CONTEXT [Security]

An IT product or system and its associated guidance documentation that is the subject of evaluation. It is most commonly associated with ISO 15408. Acronym TOE.

Target Session Identifying Handle
CONTEXT [iSCSI]

An identifier, assigned by the iSCSI target, for a session with a specific named initiator. Acronym TSIH.

TByte

Shorthand for terabyte.

TCG
CONTEXT [Security]

Acronym for Trusted Computing Group.

TCO

Acronym for Total Cost of Ownership.

TCP
CONTEXT [Network]

Acronym for Transmission Control Protocol. cf. IP.

TCP Offload Engine
CONTEXT [Networking]

A technology for improving TCP/IP performance by offloading TCP/IP processing to a Network Interface Card.

TCP/IP
CONTEXT [Network]

Shorthand for the suite of protocols that includes TCP, IP, UDP, and ICMP. This is the basic set of communication protocols used on the Internet.

tenancy
CONTEXT [Fibre Channel]

The possession of a Fibre Channel abitrated loop by a device to conduct a transaction.

terabyte

Shorthand for 1,000,000,000,000 (10^12) bytes. SNIA publications typically use the 10^12 convention commonly found in I/O literature rather than the 1,099,5111,627,776 (2^40) convention sometimes used when discussing random access memory.

test system

A collection of equipment used to perform a test. In functional and performance testing, it is generally important to clearly define the test system, and distinguish it from the system under test.

third party copy

CONTEXT [Data Recovery] [Management]

A protocol for performing tape backups using minimal server resources by copying data directly from the source device (disk or array) to the target device (tape transport) without passing through a server.

threat

CONTEXT [Security]

Any circumstance or event with the potential to harm an information system through unauthorized access, destruction, disclosure, modification of data, and/or denial of service.

throughput

The number of I/O requests satisfied per unit time. Expressed in I/O requests/second, where a request is an application request to a storage subsystem to perform a read or write operation.

throughput-intensive (application)

A request intensive application.

time server

An intelligent entity in a network that enables all nodes in the network to maintain a common time base within close tolerances.

TLS

CONTEXT [Security]

Acronym for Transport Layer Security.

TLS Record Protocol
CONTEXT [Security]

The TLS Record Protocol is a layered protocol that is used for encapsulation of various higher level protocols (such as HTTP, SMTP, etc.). Using the security parameters created by the TLS Handshake Protocol, it takes messages to be transmitted, fragments the data into manageable blocks, optionally compresses the data, applies a MAC (such as MD5 or SHA), encrypts (such as NULL, DES, 3DES, etc.), and transmits the result. Received data is decrypted, verified, decompressed, and reassembled, then delivered to higher level clients. The TLS Record Protocol is defined in RFC2246.

TLS Handshake Protocol
CONTEXT [Security]

The TLS Handshake Protocol allows peers (the server and client) to agree upon security parameters for the record layer (TLS Record Protocol), authenticate themselves (key exchange), instantiate negotiated security parameters, and report error conditions to each other before the application protocol (such as HTTP, SMTP, etc.) transmits or receives its first byte of data. The security parameters are actually created from the session identifier, certificates (X509v3), compression method, cipher spec (bulk encryption algorithm and a MAC algorithm), master secret, and resumability flag. The TLS Handshake Protocol is defined in RFC2246.

TNC
CONTEXT [Network]

Acronym for Threaded Neil Councilman, a type of Coaxial Cable Connector.

Specifications for TNC style connectors are defined in MIL-C-39012 and MIL-C-23329.

TOE
CONTEXT [Networking] [Security]

1. [Networking] Acronym for TCP Offload Engine.
2. [Security] Acronym for Target of Evaluation.

token ring (network)

CONTEXT [Network]

1. A network in which each node's transmitter is connected to the receiver of the node to its logical right, forming a continuous ring. Nodes on a token ring network gain the right to transmit data by retaining a token (a specific unique message) when they receive it. When a node holding the token has transmitted its allotment of data, it forwards the token to the next node in the ring

2. A LAN protocol for token ring networks governed by IEEE Standard 802.3 that operates at speeds of 4 Mbits/second and 16 Mbits/second.

topology

The logical layout of the components of a computer system or network and their interconnections. Topology deals with questions of what components are directly connected to other components from the standpoint of being able to communicate. It does not deal with questions of physical location of components or interconnecting cables.

total cost of ownership

The comprehensive cost of a particular capability such as data processing, storage access, file services, etc. Abbreviated TCO, total cost of ownership includes acquisition, environment, operations, management, service, upgrade, loss of service, and residual value. cf. inherent cost

TPC

CONTEXT [Data Recovery] [Management]

Acronym for third party copy.

transceiver

CONTEXT [Fibre Channel]

A transmitter and receiver combined in one package.

transmission character

CONTEXT [Fibre Channel]

Any encoded character (valid or invalid) transmitted across a physical interface specified by FC-0. Valid transmission characters are specified by the transmission code and include data characters and special characters.

transmission code

CONTEXT [Fibre Channel]

A means of encoding data to enhance its transmission characteristics. The transmission code specified by FC-PH is byte-oriented, with both valid data bytes and special codes encoded into 10-bit transmission characters.

Transmission Control Protocol

The Internet connection oriented network transport protocol. Acronym TCP. TCP provides a reliable delivery service.

transmission word

CONTEXT [Fibre Channel]

A string of four contiguous transmission characters aligned on boundaries that are zero modulo 4 from a previously received or transmitted special character. FC-1 transmission and reception operates in transmission word units.

transmitter

CONTEXT [Fibre Channel]

1. The portion of a Link_Control_Facility that converts valid data bytes and special codes into transmission characters using the rules specified by the transmission code, converting these transmission characters into a bit stream, and transmitting this bit stream on an optical or electrical transmission medium

2. An electronic circuit that converts an electrical logic signal to a signal suitable for an optical or electrical communications media.

transparent failover

A failover from one component of a system to another that is transparent to the external operating environment. Often used to refer to paired disk controllers, one of which exports the other's virtual disks at the same host bus addresses after a failure. cf. non-transparent failover.

transport layer security
CONTEXT [Security]

> A protocol that provides confidentiality and data integrity between two communicating applications. Abbreviated TLS. It is composed of two layers: the TLS Record Protocol and the TLS Handshake Protocol. The TLS Record Protocol provides connection security with an encryption method (such as DES). The TLS Handshake Protocol allows peers (client and server) to authenticate each other as well as to negotiate an encryption algorithm and cryptographic keys before data is exchanged. The TLS protocol is standardized by the Internet Engineering Task Force (IETF) and is defined in RFC2246 and related documents. TLS is based on SSL, which was designed by Netscape Communications, but TLS and SSL are not interoperable; however, the TLS protocol does contain a mechanism that allows TLS implementations to back down to SSLv3. Acronym TLS.

trap
CONTEXT [Management]

> A type of SNMP message used to signal that an event has occurred.

triaxial cable

> An electrical transmission medium consisting of three concentric conductors separated by a dielectric material with the spacings and material arranged to give a specified electrical impedance. cf. coaxial cable.

Triple DES
CONTEXT [Security]

> A variant of the Data Encryption Standard (DES) in which the algorithm is applied three times in succession using two or three different keys. Acronym 3DES.

trojan horse
CONTEXT [Security]

> A computer program containing hidden code that allows the unauthorized collection, falsification, or destruction of information.

trust

CONTEXT [Security]

> Belief in the reliability, truth, ability, or strength of someone or something. Assured reliance on the ability of a system to function as expected and to not misbehave. (The belief that a system will do what it supposed to do and not do what it is not supposed to do.)

Trusted Computing Group

CONTEXT [Security]

> A not-for-profit organization formed to develop, define, and promote open standards for hardware-enabled trusted computing and security technologies, including hardware building blocks and software interfaces, across multiple platforms, peripherals, and devices. Acronym TCG.

T

trusted system

CONTEXT [Security]

> A system that employs sufficient hardware and software integrity measures to assure that it performs according to its documented specification and acts in a predictable manner which may be used for processing of sensitive or classified information. Such a system is developed in accordance with security criteria and evaluated by these criteria.

TSIH

CONTEXT [iSCSI]

> Acronym for Target Session Identifying Handle.

tunneling

CONTEXT [Security]

> A technology that enables one network protocol to send its data via another network protocol's connections. Tunneling works by encapsulating the first network protocol within packets carried by the second protocol. A tunnel may also encapsulate a protocol within itself (e.g., an IPsec gateway operates in this fashion, encapsulating IP in IP and inserting additional IPsec information between the two IP headers).

UDP
CONTEXT [Network]

Acronym for User Datagram Protocol.

ULP
CONTEXT [Fibre Channel]

Acronym for Upper Layer Protocol.

Ultra SCSI
CONTEXT [SCSI]

A form of SCSI capable of 20 megatransfers per second. Single ended Ultra SCSI supports bus lengths of up to 1.5 meters. Differential Ultra SCSI supports bus lengths of up to 25 meters. Ultra SCSI specifications define both narrow (8 data bits) and wide (16 data bits) buses. A narrow Ultra SCSI bus transfers data at a maximum of 20 MBytes per second. A wide Ultra SCSI bus transfers data at a maximum of 40 MBytes per second.

Ultra2 SCSI
CONTEXT [SCSI]

A form of SCSI capable of 40 megatransfers per second. There is no single ended Ultra2 SCSI specification. Low voltage differential (LVD) Ultra2 SCSI supports bus lengths of up to 12 meters. High voltage differential Ultra2 SCSI supports bus lengths of up to 25 meters. Ultra2 SCSI specifications define both narrow (8 data bits) and wide (16 data bits) buses. A narrow Ultra SCSI bus transfers data at a maximum of 40 MBytes per second. A wide Ultra2 SCSI bus transfers data at a maximum of 80 MBytes per second.

Ultra3 SCSI

CONTEXT [SCSI]

A form of SCSI capable of 80 megatransfers per second. There is no single ended Ultra3 SCSI specification. Low voltage differential (LVD) Ultra2 SCSI supports bus lengths of up to 12 meters. There is no high voltage differential Ultra3 SCSI specification. Ultra3 SCSI specifications only define wide (16 data bits) buses. A wide Ultra3 SCSI bus transfers data at a maximum of 160 MBytes per second.

UML

CONTEXT [Management]

Acronym for Unified Modeling Language.

unauthorized disclosure

CONTEXT [Security]

The exposure of information to individuals not authorized to receive or access it.

unclassified

CONTEXT [Security]

Information that is not designated as classified

unicast

CONTEXT [Network]

The transmission of a message a single receivers. Unicast can be contrasted with broadcast (sending a message to all receivers on a network) and multicast (sending a message to select subset of receivers).

Unicode

A standard for a 16-bit character set (each character has a 16-bit number associated with it). Unicode allows for up to 2^16, or 65,536 characters, each of which may have a unique representation. It accommodates several non-English characters and symbols, and is therefore an aid to development of products with multilingual user interfaces. Unicode was designed and is maintained by the non-profit industry consortium Unicode Inc.

uninterruptible power source

A source of electrical power that is not affected by outages in a building's external power source. Abbreviated UPS. UPSs may generate their own power using gasoline generators, or they may consist of large banks of batteries. UPSs are typically installed to prevent service outages due to external power grid failure in computer applications deemed by their owners to be "mission critical."

Unified Modeling Language

CONTEXT [Management]

A visual approach that uses a variety of diagrams such as use case, class, interaction, state, activity and others) to specify the objects of a model and their relationships. Abbreviated UML. Various tools exist for turning UML diagrams into program code.

unsolicited control

CONTEXT [Fibre Channel]

An information category indicated in a Fibre Channel frame header.

unsolicited data

CONTEXT [Fibre Channel]

An information category indicated in a Fibre Channel frame header.

upper layer protocol

CONTEXT [Fibre Channel]

A protocol used on a Fibre Channel network at or above the FC-4 level. Abbreviated ULP. SCSI and IP are examples of ULPs.

UPS

Acronym for Uninterruptible Power Source.

usable capacity

CONTEXT [Storage Device] [Storage System]

The storage capacity in a disk or disk array that is available for storing user data. Usable capacity of a disk is the total formatted capacity of a disk minus the capacity reserved for media defect compensation and meta-data. Usable capacity of a disk array is the sum of the usable capacities of the array's member disks minus the capacity required for check data and metadata.

user data extent

CONTEXT [Storage System]

> The protected space in one or more contiguously located redundancy group stripes in a single redundancy group. In RAID arrays, collections of user data extents comprise the virtual disks or volume sets presented to the operating environment.

user data extent stripe depth

CONTEXT [Storage System]

> The number of consecutive blocks of protected space in a single user data extent that are mapped to consecutive virtual disk block addresses. In principle, each user data extent that is part of a virtual disk may have a different user data extent stripe depth. User data extent stripe depth may differ from the redundancy group stripe depth of the protected space extent in which it resides.

User Datagram Protocol

CONTEXT [Network]

> An Internet protocol that provides connectionless datagram delivery service to applications. Abbreviated UDP. UDP over IP adds the ability to address multiple endpoints within a single network node to IP.

user identification number

> A unique number that identifies an individual to a computer system. Abbreviated UID. UIDs are the result of authentication processes that use account names, passwords and possibly other data to verify that a user is actually who she represents herself to be. UIDs are input to authorization processes that grant or deny access to resources based on the identification of the requesting user.

V

valid data byte
CONTEXT [Fibre Channel]

A string of eight contiguous bits within FC-1 which represents a value between 0 and 255.

valid frame
CONTEXT [Fibre Channel]

A received frame containing a valid Start_of_Frame (SOF), a valid End_of_Frame (EOF), valid data characters, and proper Cyclic Redundancy Check (CRC) of the Frame Header and Data Field.

validity control bit
CONTEXT [Fibre Channel]

A control bit that indicates whether a field is valid. If a validity control bit indicates that a field is invalid, the value in the field is treated as invalid.

VBA
CONTEXT [Storage System]

Acronym for Virtual Block Address.

VCI

Acronym for Virtual Channel Identifier.

VCSEL

CONTEXT [Fibre Channel]

Acronym for Vertical Cavity Surface Emitting Laser.

vendor unique

CONTEXT [Standards]

Aspects of a standard (e.g., functions, codes, etc.) not defined by the standard, but explicitly reserved for private usage between parties using the standard. Different implementations of a standard may assign different meanings to vendor unique aspects of the standard.

verify

verification

CONTEXT [Data Recovery]

The object-by-object comparison of the contents of a backup image with the online data objects from which it was made.

versioning

CONTEXT [Data Recovery]

The maintenance of multiple point-in-time copies of a collection of data. Versioning is used to minimize recovery time by increasing the number of intermediate checkpoints from which an application can be restarted.

Vertical Cavity Surface Emitting Laser

CONTEXT [Fibre Channel]

A surface emitting laser source fabricated on a planar wafer with emission perpendicular to the wafer.

VI

Acronym for Virtual Interface (Architecture)

VIA

Acronym for Virtual Interface Architecture.

virtual block

CONTEXT [Storage System]

A block in the address space presented by a virtual disk. Virtual blocks are the atomic units in which a virtual disk's storage capacity is typically presented by RAID arrays to their operating environments.

virtual block address

CONTEXT [Storage System]

The address of a virtual block. Virtual block addresses are typically used in hosts' I/O commands addressed to the virtual disks instantiated by RAID arrays. SCSI disk commands addressed to RAID arrays, are actually using virtual block addresses in their logical block address fields.

virtual channel identifier

CONTEXT [Network]

A unique numerical tag contained in an ATM cell header. Acronym VCI. A VCI identifies an ATM virtual channel over which the cell containing it is to travel.

virtual circuit

CONTEXT [Fibre Channel]

1. A set of state information shared by two communicating nodes that is independent of the particular path taken by any particular transmission
2. A unidirectional path between two communicating N_Ports. Fibre Channel virtual circuits may be limited to a fraction of the bandwidth available on the physical link.

virtual device

CONTEXT [Storage System]

A device presented to an operating environment by control software or by a volume manager. From an application standpoint, a virtual device is equivalent to a physical one. In some implementations, virtual devices may differ from physical ones at the operating system level (e.g., booting from a host based disk array may not be possible).

virtual disk

CONTEXT [Storage System]

A set of disk blocks presented to an operating environment as a range of consecutively numbered logical blocks with disk-like storage and I/O semantics. The virtual disk is the disk array object that most closely resembles a physical disk from the operating environment's viewpoint. cf. logical disk.

Virtual Interface Architecture

An API specification for direct communication among distributed applications developed by Intel, Compaq, and Microsoft. Abbreviated VIA. VIA reduces interprocess communication latency by obviating the need for applications to use processor interrupt or operating system paths to intercommunicate, while maintaining security on the communications path. VIA is interconnect neutral. cf. Fibre Channel Virtual Interface.

virtual path identifier

CONTEXT [Network]
An eight-bit field in an ATM cell header that denotes the cell over which the cell should be routed.

virtual tape

CONTEXT [Storage System]

A virtual device with the characteristics of a tape.

virtualization

The act of integrating one or more (back end) services or functions with additional (front end) functionality for the purpose of providing useful abstractions. Typically virtualization hides some of the back end complexity, or adds or integrates new functionality with existing back end services. Examples of virtualization are the aggregation of multiple instances of a service into one virtualized service, or to add security to an otherwise insecure service. Virtualization can be nested or applied to multiple layers of a system.

virus

CONTEXT [Security]

A type of programmed threat. A code fragment (not an independent program) that replicates by attaching to another program, and either damaging information directly or causing denial of service

volatility

A property of data. Volatility refers to the certainty that data will be obliterated if certain environmental conditions are not met. For example, data held in DRAM is volatile, since if electrical power to DRAM is cut, the data in it is obliterated. cf. non-volatility, persistence

volume

CONTEXT [Storage System]

1. for virtual disk. Used to denote virtual disks created by volume manager control software.
2. A piece of removable media that has been prepared for use by a backup manager (e.g., by the writing of a media ID).

volume group

CONTEXT [Data Recovery]

A collection of removable media that reside in a single location, for example in a single robot or group of interconnected robots.

volume manager

CONTEXT [Storage System]

Common term for host-based control software.

volume pool

CONTEXT [Data Recovery]

A logical collection of removable media designated for a given purpose, for example, for holding the copies of a single repetitive backup job, or for backing up data from a given client or set of clients. A volume pool is an administrative entity, whereas a volume group is a physical one.

volume set

CONTEXT [Storage System]

Synonym for virtual disk.

VPI

Acronym for Virtual Path Identifier.

vulnerability

CONTEXT [Security]

A weakness in an information system, system security procedures, internal controls, or implementation that could be exploited.

V

WAN
CONTEXT [Network]

Acronym for Wide Area Network.

warm spare (disk)
CONTEXT [Storage System]

A spare to which power is applied, and which is not operating, but which is otherwise usable as a hot spare.

warm swap

The substitution of a replacement unit (RU) in a system for a defective one, where in order to perform the substitution, the system must be stopped (caused to cease performing its function), but power need not be removed. Warm swaps are manual (performed by humans) physical operations—cf. automatic swap, cold swap, hot swap.

Wave Division Multiplexing

The splitting of light into a series of "colors" from a few (sparse) to many with a narrow wavelength separation (Dense WDM) for the purpose of carrying simultaneous traffic over the same physical fiber (9 micron usually). Each "color" is a separate data stream.

WBEM
CONTEXT [Management]

> Acronym for Web Based Enterprise Management

WDM
CONTEXT [Windows]

> Acronym for Wave Division Multiplexing.
> Acronym for Windows Driver Model.

Web Based Enterprise Management
CONTEXT [Management]

> Web-Based Enterprise Management is an initiative in the DMTF.
> Abbreviated WBEM. It is a set of technologies that enables interoperable
> management of an enterprise. WBEM consists of CIM, an XML DTD defining
> the tags (XML encodings) to describe the CIM Schema and its data, and a
> set of HTTP operations for exchanging the XML-based information. CIM
> joins the XML data description language and HTTP transport protocol
> with an underlying information model, CIM to create a conceptual view of
> the enterprise.

well-known address
CONTEXT [Fibre Channel]

> An address identifier used to access a service provided by a Fibre
> Channel fabric. A well-known address is not subject to zone restrictions;
> i.e., a well-known address is always accessible, irrespective of the
> current active zone set.

wide SCSI
CONTEXT [SCSI]

> Any form of SCSI using a 16-bit data path. In a wide SCSI implementation,
> the data transfer rate in MBytes per second is twice the number of mega-
> transfers per second because each transfer cycle transfers two bytes. cf.
> fast SCSI, Ultra SCSI, Ultra2 SCSI, Ultra3 SCSI.

wide area network
CONTEXT [Network]

> A a communications network that is geographically dispersed and that
> includes telecommunications links. Acronym WAN.

Windows Driver Model

CONTEXT [Windows]

A Microsoft specification for device drivers to operate in both the Windows NT and Windows 95/98 operating systems.

Windows Internet Naming Service

CONTEXT [Windows]

A facility of the Windows NT operating system that translates between IP addresses and symbolic names for network nodes and resources. Acronym WINS.

Windows Management Instrumentation

CONTEXT [Windows]

The name of the Microsoft framework that supports CIM and WBEM. A set of Windows NT operating system facilities that enable operating system components to provide management information to management agents. Acronym WMI.

WINS

CONTEXT [Windows]

Acronym for Windows Internet Naming Service.

WMI

CONTEXT [Windows]

Acronym for Windows Management Instrumentation.

word

CONTEXT [General] [Fibre Channel]

1. An addressable unit of data in computer memory. Typically defined to be 16 consecutively addressed bits. Most processor architectures include arithmetic and logical instructions that operate on words.
2. [Fibre Channel] The smallest Fibre Channel data element consisting of 40 serial bits representing either a flag (K28.5) plus three encoded data bytes (ten encoded bits each) or four ten bit encoded data bytes.
3. [Fibre Channel] A string of four contiguous bytes occurring on boundaries that are zero modulo four from a specified reference. cf. transmission word

workgroup

A group of UNIX or Windows computer system users, usually with a common mission or project, that is created for administrative simplicity.

World Wide Name (WWN)

CONTEXT [Fibre Channel]

1. A 64-bit unsigned Name_Identifier which is worldwide unique. cf. Fibre Channel Name
2. A unique 64 bit number assigned by a recognized naming authority (often via block assignment to a manufacturer) that identifies a node process or node port. See WWNN and WWPN. Abbreviated WWN. A WWN is assigned for the life of a connection (device). Most networking physical transport network technologies use a world wide unique identifier convention. For example, the Ethernet Media Access Control Identifier, often referred to as the MAC address.

World Wide Node Name (WWNN)

CONTEXT [Fibre Channel]

A globally unique 64-bit identifier assigned for each Upper Layer node process mapped by Fibre Channel.

World Wide Port Name (WWPN)

CONTEXT [Fibre Channel]

A globally unique 64-bit identifier assigned to each Fibre Channel port. Fibre Channel ports' WWPN are permitted to use any of several naming authorities. Fibre Channel specifies a Network Address Authority (NAA) to distinguish between the various name registration authorities that may be used to identify the WWPN.

worm

CONTEXT [Security]

An independent program that replicates from computer to computer across network connections, often clogging networks and computer systems as it spreads.

write hole
CONTEXT [Storage System]

A potential data corruption problem for parity RAID technology resulting from an array failure while application I/O is outstanding, followed by an unrelated member disk failure (some time after the array has been returned to service). Data corruption can occur if member data and parity become inconsistent due to the array failure, resulting in a false regeneration when data from the failed member disk is subsequently requested by an application. Parity RAID implementations typically include mechanisms eliminate the possibility of write holes.

write back cache

A caching technique in which the completion of a write request is signaled as soon as the data is in cache, and actual writing to non-volatile media occurs at a later time. Write-back cache includes an inherent risk that an application will take some action predicated on the write completion signal, and a system failure before the data is written to non-volatile media will cause media contents to be inconsistent with that subsequent action. For this reason, good write-back cache implementations include mechanisms to preserve cache contents across system failures (including power failures) and to flush the cache at system restart time. cf. write through cache

W

write penalty

Low apparent application write performance to independent access RAID arrays' virtual disks. The write penalty is inherent in independent access RAID data protection techniques, which require multiple member I/O requests for each application write request, and ranges from minimal (mirrored arrays) to substantial (RAID Levels 5 and 6). Many RAID array designs include features such as write-back cache specifically to minimize the write penalty.

write through cache

A caching technique in which the completion of a write request is not signaled until data is safely stored on non-volatile media. Write performance with a write-through cache is approximately that of a non-cached system, but if the data written is also held in cache, subsequent read performance may be dramatically improved. cf. write back cache

X_ID

CONTEXT [Fibre Channel]

> Acronym for Exchange_Identifier.

X3T10

CONTEXT [SCSI]

> The ANSI X3T10 technical committee, the standards organization responsible for SCSI standards for communication between computers and storage subsystems and devices.

X3T11

CONTEXT [Fibre Channel]

> The ANSI X3T11 technical committee, the standards organization responsible for Fibre Channel and certain other standards for moving electronic data in and out of computers.

XML

> Acronym for eXtensible Markup Language.

zero filling
CONTEXT [Security]

> The process of filling unused storage locations in an information system with the representation of the character denoting "0".

zeroization
CONTEXT [Security]

> The process of removing or eliminating the key from a cryptographic program or device.

zone
CONTEXT [Fibre Channel]

> A collection of Fibre Channel N_Ports and/or NL_Ports (i.e., device ports) that are permitted to communicate with each other via the fabric. Any two N_Ports and/or NL_Ports that are not members of at least one common zone are not permitted to communicate via the fabric. Zone membership may be specified by: 1) port location on a switch, (i.e., Domain_ID and port number); or, 2) the device's N_Port_Name; or, 3) the device's address identifier; or, 4) the device's Node_Name. Well-known addresses are implicitly included in every zone.

zone set
CONTEXT [Fibre Channel]

> A set of zone definitions for a fabric. Zones in a zone set may overlap (i.e., a port may be a member of more than one zone). Fabric management may support switching between zone sets to enforce different access restrictions (e.g., at different times of day).

zoning
CONTEXT [Fibre Channel]

> A method of subdividing a storage area network into disjoint zones, or subsets of nodes on the network. Storage area network nodes outside a zone are invisible to nodes within the zone. Moreover, with switched SANs, traffic within each zone may be physically isolated from traffic outside the zone.

3DES

CONTEXT [Security]

> Acronym for Triple DES.

8B/10B encoding

CONTEXT [Fibre Channel]

> An algorithm for encoding data for transmission in which each eight-bit data byte is converted to a 10-bit transmission character. Invented and patented by IBM Corporation, 8B/10B encoding is used in transmitting data on Fibre Channel, ESCON, and Gigabit Ethernet.8B/10B encoding supports continuous transmission with a balanced number of ones and zeros in the code stream and detects single bit transmission errors.

\#

The The Storage Networking Industry Association (SNIA)
would like to thank the following sponsors
for making this version of the dictionary possible.

www.cisco.com/go/storagenetworking

Computer Associates®

www.ca.com/brightstor

www.equallogic.com

www.hp.com/storage

www.ibm.com/storage

www.intel.com/design/intarch/
platforms/storage/index.htm

If your organization is a SNIA member and interested in sponsoring
the 2006/2007 edition of this dictionary, please contact
Derek Jenkins at Derek.Jenkins@snia.org

Storage Networking Industry Association

500 Sansome Street, Suite 504
San Francisco, CA 94111
Phone: 415-402-0006

www.snia.org